Living FOR Today

Planning FOR Tomorrow

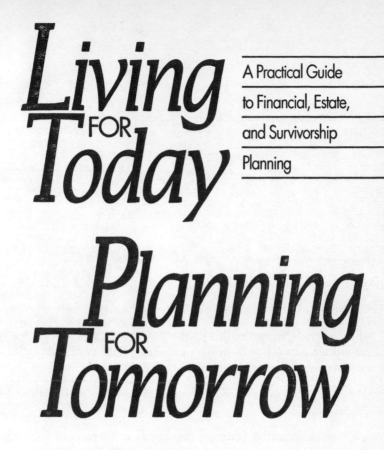

Living FOR *Today*

A Practical Guide
to Financial, Estate,
and Survivorship
Planning

Planning FOR *Tomorrow*

Shelly Lynch

World Wide Publications
A ministry of the Billy Graham Evangelistic Association
1303 Hennepin Ave., Minneapolis, Minnesota 55403

Living for Today / Planning for Tomorrow

© 1989, 1996 Billy Graham Evangelistic Association

World Wide Publications is the publishing ministry of the Billy Graham Evangelistic Association.

Unless otherwise indicated, Scripture quotations are taken from The Holy Bible, New International Version. Copyright © 1973, 1978, 1984 International Bible Society. Used by permission of Zondervan Bible Publishers.

Scripture quotations marked KJV are taken from the Authorized King James Version of the Bible.

Scripture quotations marked TLB are taken from The Living Bible, © 1971 Tyndale House Publishers. Used by permission.

Scripture quotations marked NASB are taken from the New American Standard Bible, © 1960, 1962, 1963, 1968, 1971, 1972, 1973, 1975, 1977 The Lockman Foundation, La Habra, California.

ISBN: 0-89066-176-6

Library of Congress Catalog Card Number: 89-050478

Printed in the United States of America

Contents

Acknowledgments

My sincere thanks and deep appreciation to:

My husband, Brian, who daily shares his strength and love with me.

Jack Richardson, Director of Development Ministries for the Billy Graham Evangelistic Association and my boss, who from the beginning saw the need for this book and encouraged me to do the research and writing and who willingly reviewed each draft. Jack has been a certified public accountant for more than thirty-two years. For the past twenty-six years he has been active in the deferred giving field in administrative and management positions.

John Vanderbeck, Associate Director, who willingly provided the research for "Housing Options," chapter 6, from his twenty years of experience in this field. John is past president of National Housing Ministries (a retirement housing development and management corporation). He earned his doctoral degree from Judson College, an advanced management degree from Harvard, and his theological degree from North American Baptist Seminary. He has pastored four churches. He is listed in *Who's Who in the Midwest*, *Who's Who in Religion*, and *The Dictionary of International Biography*. Also, he has published numerous sermons and professional articles.

Ronald Simers, Operations Manager, who offered his expertise in reviewing "Financial Planning," chapter 1, and "Estate Planning," chapter 2. Ron earned his B.S. degree in Business Administration from the University of Akron (Ohio). He attended Philanthropy Tax Institute Deferred Giving Seminars and Kennedy Sinclaire Inc. Planned Gifts Program. He is past trust accountant with the Church of the Nazarene headquarters in Kansas City, Missouri. He is listed in *Who's Who in the Midwest* and *Outstanding Young Men of America.*

Stephen G. Scholle, J.D., who reviewed the manuscript for technical and legal accuracy. Steve is Legal Counsel with the Billy Graham Evangelistic Association. He is a member of the Hennepin County and Minnesota Bar Associations, licensed to practice in Minnesota and federal courts. He is also a member of the probate and estates committee with Hennepin County.

Stephen Griffith, Publishing and Marketing Manager for World Wide Publications, Bill Deckard, my editor, and Helen Hanson, my special editorial consultant, all of whom helped shape the manuscript into its final form.

Co-workers who have supported and encouraged me in many ways.

The nurses, doctors, and pastors whom I will always remember because of their loving care for me during my hospitalization when we lost our son.

Our family and friends whose constant love and concern for Brian and me was so evident during our time of sorrow.

In loving memory of our firstborn son, Samuel Leon Lynch, who was born and died on November 13, 1988.

"I prayed for this child, and the Lord has granted me what I asked of him. So now I give him to the Lord. For his whole life he will be given over to the Lord."

—1 Samuel 1:27-28

Introduction

This book is written as a practical guide to help people through two stages of life: planning an estate and settling an estate. For many people these are difficult areas to face.

Through our work with Development Ministries of the Billy Graham Evangelistic Association, we know the importance of estate planning. Unfortunately, its importance is generally more evident to the survivors when it is too late. It is our hope that this book will encourage you to take steps to plan your estate and even to pre-plan your funeral arrangements. We trust it will give you a new perspective on estate planning—not to focus on your death but to see it as a future gift to your survivors during a time of great need.

Settling an estate is seldom easy. Many critical decisions must be made during an extremely stressful and emotional time. The task can seem overwhelming—especially if it is the first time you've had to experience this. We hope that this book will serve as a "friend" to help you through the necessary decisions, and that having this guide will be of comfort by helping to relieve some of the stress as you make so many important decisions.

Much of this book is information and facts accumulated through our staff's experience in helping many individuals with both estate planning and estate settlement. We saw a need to present this material in one book in an organized and concise arrangement. Of course we cannot cover every aspect of financial, estate, and survivorship planning as these are broad topics. Hopefully if you have questions that are not addressed within the text of the book, the list of additional resources (see pages 163-76) will be of help. Also, we hope it will be evident that we are concerned with addressing issues of the heart as well as presenting guides and facts.

We trust that the information contained in the following pages will minister to you in settling an estate as you live for today during a time of personal sorrow, and that it will help you as you plan for tomorrow as a gift to your survivors.

Part I
Planning Ahead

1
Financial Planning: Who Can Help Me?

"We should make plans—counting on God to direct us."
(Proverbs 16:9, TLB)

Failure to plan ahead has caused irreversible problems for many people in their later years. Some have arrived at retirement without pensions or other income. Some find themselves without protection against inflation or without adequate health and disability insurance. Many problems can be avoided by planning ahead. And it will help bring peace of mind knowing you are prepared for the future.

Financial and estate planning is a step-by-step process that takes time and careful consideration. It is not a one-time event but rather an ongoing process—but it is worth the effort! It is important to identify your future needs and goals and to continually review and revise your plans as necessary. Because there are a number of issues to consider in financial and estate planning, the earlier you begin to plan, the better.

You may be asking, "How do I begin the financial and estate planning process?" Following are some guidelines to keep in mind as you plan for your future:

1. Be informed. You have already taken a big step in this area by reading this or other books of this nature. Gather and read information on all aspects of financial and estate planning: investment tools, Social Security, insurance, survivors' benefits, funeral planning, housing, etc.

2. Talk with others. You can learn much just by talking with others. Also, talk with your spouse or loved ones who will be affected by your decisions.

3. Set goals. Establish realistic goals for your future based on your needs and desires. Pray and ask the Lord to direct your decision-making.

4. Keep a written record. An important part of financial and estate planning is putting your plans in writing. This will enable you to review and revise your plans as your goals and resources change.

5. Review and revise. Review your financial and estate plans on a yearly basis—or more often, as your needs, circumstances, and resources change. Mark the "review date" on your calendar. Failure to review at least once a year may result in unforeseen problems down the road which could have been avoided.

An important part of financial and estate planning is working toward financial security. Financial security in your retirement years begins by establishing a sound financial plan now—whether you are two, ten, or twenty years away from retirement.

Biblical Financial Planning

Some people question whether the Bible condones establishing a financial plan for their lives. They wonder whether preparing a financial plan is in contradiction to living by faith in a God who supplies our daily needs. When we make plans without God, then we are acting in disobedience. However, the Lord has given us the responsibility to be wise stewards of that which he has entrusted to us including our time, talents, and tangible goods.

Everything we have rightfully belongs to God. He is the owner. We are the managers. The Bible says, "The earth is the Lord's, and the fulness thereof; the world, and they that dwell therein" (Psalm 24:1, KJV). It also says, "The silver is mine, and the gold is mine, saith the Lord of hosts" (Haggai 2:8, KJV).

In 1 Timothy 6:10 (KJV) Paul writes, "For the love of money is the root of all evil: which while some coveted after, they have erred from the faith, and pierced themselves through with many sorrows." Note that it is not money itself but the *love* of money, that is evil. God looks at the attitude of the heart.

It is a biblical principle to be a wise steward of the money we manage for the Lord. To be a wise steward involves planning and investing that which we are given so that there will be an increase which may be used for his glory.

Biblical financial planning is a partnership between God and man. God supplies the capital, and man supplies the labor. God gives us wisdom, strength, power, and the means to work and save. Men and women must be obedient to do the work God has given them, whatever that work may be. In order to establish a wise financial plan, you will need to begin by gathering information.

Gathering Information

The first step in the information gathering process is to list your assets. In order to compile a list of your assets, you may want to take a tape recorder or dictaphone and walk through your house, garage, and office. Describe the things you own and give an estimated value for each item. When you've made a complete accounting, transcribe the tape (or have someone do this for you) so you will have a written copy of your assets. If you take a little extra time while making the recording, you can make a valuable resource for your family by stating how and when to care for each item.

You will probably be pleasantly surprised as you add up your list. Most people are worth more than they think, particularly when they consider the value of their home and pension. Be sure to update this list yearly as you purchase new items. Should you sell or give anything away, be sure to remove it from your list. It may be helpful to your survivors to indicate what you have done with the item(s). Your survivors will appreciate receiving written instructions on how to care for your personal belongings and various assets.

Getting Your Papers in Order

Having gathered information about your tangible assets, the next step is to make sure your papers are in order. You will want to do this before your initial meeting with financial and estate planners. You will save both time and expense, since attorneys and other professional advisors base their fees on an hourly rate. It will be helpful to your survivors as well to have your important papers completed and filed in an organized manner. You may choose to have your papers filed in folders in a metal file cabinet preferably with a lock. (Be sure to tell the person who will be the executor of your estate where the key may be found.) It is useful to store previous years' papers in separate boxes with the year written on each box.

These papers will give your planners and survivors the valuable information they will need to know regarding your personal and financial affairs. You can be of great assistance to your survivors *now* by keeping them informed about every aspect of your personal and financial affairs including mortgages, debts, contracts, trusts, wills, stocks and bonds, property (tangible or intangible), any assets you may own, the normal utility and general household operating costs, your bank accounts, and so on. This familiarity will help your survivors settle your estate more easily when the time comes.

Setting Up a Records Book

Even though you may have your important papers completed and organized, the information your planners and survivors will need to know may be on various forms and documents. It is extremely helpful to have your vital information contained in one place, such as a records book, so that your planners and survivors will be able to find the specific information they need quickly, rather than searching through your files. There are many types of records books available for this purpose. You may want to check your local office supply store or bookstore to purchase a records book. (See appendix A, pages 137-48 for a list of the information to be contained in your records book.)

Financial and Estate Planning Team

Survivors are faced with many decisions at one of the most difficult times in their lives and often with little or no preparation. You can show love and concern by preparing them to handle the responsibilities accompanying your death. "A prudent man foresees the difficulties ahead and prepares for them; the simpleton goes blindly on and suffers the consequences" (Proverbs 22:3, TLB).

Your survivors may ask, "What do I do? Who can I turn to for help?" It is important that your survivors know whom they can turn to when they need sound financial or legal advice. You may want to do some research in advance to compile a list of the names and addresses of reliable professionals whom you (and your survivors) can contact for advice. Be sure to list their names, addresses, and telephone numbers, and their areas of expertise. "Plans go wrong with too few counselors; many counselors bring success" (Proverbs 15:22, TLB).

You will want your financial and estate planning team to consist of as many of the following professionals as the size of your estate requires:

Attorney: To assist you in legal matters such as preparing your will and other legal documents, and probate.

Certified public accountant (CPA): To assist you with regard to taxes and investments.

Certified financial planner (CFP): To assist you with regard to investments and tax implications.

Bank manager: To assist you in compiling a list of the estate assets and to provide a number of financial services.

Trust officer: To assist you in compiling a list of the estate assets and to assist in preparing a trust agreement.

Stockbroker: To provide a variety of investment vehicles such as stocks, bonds, money markets, and mutual funds.

Real estate agent: To assist with property investments which have tax advantages and long or short-term growth.

Life insurance underwriter: To assist you in completing claims for life insurance benefits and in evaluating your future insurance needs.

Health insurance agent: To review current protection and to suggest health and disability insurance for future needs.

Selecting Your Team Members

The best way to find good financial and estate planners is to receive recommendations from others. Ask your friends, co-workers, and family members for a list of experts *they* trust. Then interview several planners to compare their expertise, methods, and fees as you decide whom to include on your team. Here are some questions you may want to ask them:

1. What are your areas of expertise?
2. What is your background or training?
3. What are your professional affiliations?
4. How do you keep up to date on what is happening in your field?
5. Upon what do you base your fees?
6. What do your services include? What is not included?
7. How do you prefer to work with other financial and estate planning professionals?
8. What kind of information do you need to know about me and my family?
9. Will I be working primarily with you, someone else, or

several others from your firm?
10. What are your credentials? Are you registered with the state or province?

Financial Planning

Financial planning involves three main areas: income, investments, and insurance. In establishing a well-rounded financial plan, you will need to consider all three. Otherwise, your financial plan will be incomplete. We will look briefly at these three aspects of financial planning.

Income

The first part of your financial plan is your current and future income. In establishing your financial plan, you should consider all possible sources of income and how the yield from these may be increased before and after retirement. Following are some possible sources of retirement income which may be available to you:

1. *Social Security*. Social Security is a main source of income for many retirees, but, generally, it won't provide all of the income you will need. Social Security income is normally exempt from federal income tax, but there is a limit to the amount of wages or salaries you can receive yearly after retirement without losing any Social Security benefits (see chapter 5, pages 82-3 for additional information). However, there is currently no limit on the amount of income you may receive from pensions, interest or dividends, or profits from investments.

The size of your Social Security checks depends upon the age at which you begin to draw the benefits, and the amount of your earnings covered by Social Security. You will want to check with your local Social Security office to request a statement of your earnings to date. Simply ask for the "Request for Statement of Earnings" form (see appendix B, page 149). If you are fifty-five or older, you may want to ask for an estimate of what your benefits will be at retirement. Remember, the amount will vary according to your age at the time you choose to begin receiving benefits. And even if you haven't worked outside the home and paid into the Social Security fund, you may be entitled to your spouse's benefits if you are a widow or widower. Be sure to contact your local Social Security office several months prior to your retirement to ask what information will be required in order to apply for Social Security benefits.

2. Pension plans. You should check with your company's human resources department to obtain a booklet explaining its pension plan. In order to establish your financial plan, you will need to thoroughly understand the provisions which are included and those which are not. If you are self-employed you are eligible for a Keogh plan.

3. IRAs and Keoghs. Individual Retirement Accounts (IRAs) and a Keogh plan are plans you establish yourself. By regularly putting a small sum of money into your IRA, you will be able to save a substantial amount for your retirement needs. There are many types of IRAs and Keoghs available today. You will want to do some research with various financial institutions (banks, savings and loans, stock brokerage firms, insurance companies, and mutual funds) to find the best rate of income for your long-term IRA or Keogh investment.

There are three main benefits of IRAs: (1) Within certain limits, there is no federal income tax on the contributions you put into your IRA. However, should you withdraw any funds before the allotted time, there will normally be a penalty; (2) Income you earn from your IRA is tax-free during your working years; (3) Generally, you will be in a lower tax bracket when you start to withdraw funds from your IRA, therefore the amount of tax you pay on this income will normally be reduced.

4. Savings accounts. Passbook savings accounts generally pay a lower interest rate. In times of high inflation, passbook savings accounts are not the best investment vehicle. They are fine for establishing a reserve fund should an emergency arise. However, you will want to consider higher-interest-yielding alternatives, such as money market funds and certificates of deposit (CDs), for your investments. Your financial planners will be able to assist you in making sound investments.

5. Employment. Another source of retirement income to consider may be a part-time job or your own business. Some prospective employers will consider your age to be a negative factor. However, you may have a lot of experience to offer, and this will be a plus in your favor. If you want to start your own small business at retirement, you will want to begin planning well ahead of time.

Investments

The second important part of financial planning is your investment plan. There are many types of investment vehicles available today. Your CPA, CFP, or stockbroker will be able to assist you in meeting your investment goals and objectives. Investment tools include:

1. Common stocks. These are shares of ownership in a company. Stocks pay dividends. Stocks can increase or decrease in value depending upon the company's growth or loss in net profits and market conditions.

2. *Preferred stocks.* These are shares of ownership in a company which pay a fixed dividend and are paid before any dividends are distributed to common stockholders. Generally, they have little growth potential.

3. *U.S. Government and corporate bonds.* U.S. Government bonds are backed by the federal government and have generally been considered a good investment. Long-term federal government obligations are called *bonds*, intermediate-term are called *notes*, and short-term are called *bills*. Corporate bonds are graded by bond-rating services. Bonds fluctuate in value, but at maturity they are redeemed at face value.

4. *Municipal bonds.* These bonds are issued by municipalities from towns, cities, counties, and states. They are generally exempt from federal taxes and usually have lower yields than taxable bonds.

5. *Mutual bonds.* You can buy shares in a professionally managed fund which invests in various kinds of securities according to the fund's objective. Some funds are designed for growth (long-term) and others for income (short-term). This allows for greater diversification as the fund invests in many securities. You will want to make sure the fund is sound before you invest.

6. *Annuities.* These are contracts sold by insurance companies that guarantee the annuitant a fixed income for life or a certain number of years. They offer steady income but no growth potential. Charitable gift annuities differ from commercial annuities in that, with a gift annuity, a portion of the money is applied to the annuity and a portion is given to the organization as a gift (for which you receive a charitable contribution deduction).

7. *Real estate.* Your own home may be one of your best investments as real estate generally increases in value over the years. Plus, you will be entitled to claim a one-time capital gains tax exemption if you sell your home after age fifty-five, subject to certain restrictions.

Apartment buildings, business property, or rental houses can provide an income for you, as well as some tax advantages. However, it will involve a certain amount of responsibility and management. Your real estate advisor will be able to assist you should you wish to consider investing in real estate.

Before you make an investment, you will want to define your investment objective. Do you want maximum growth of your principal, or do you want a current high income yield? Do you want a long or short-term investment? (See Investment Objective chart in appendix C, page 150).

Another investment guideline is not to "put all your eggs in one basket"—diversify. Seek balance. When investing, you may want to consider putting some of your assets into a "risk" program while putting the rest of your assets into fixed-return or "safe" investments.

Equally as important as *where* you invest your assets is *whom* you invest them with. Be sure your investment advisor (CPA, CFP, stockbroker) is trustworthy and reliable. Be aware of con artists (see chapter 2) and don't be pushed into any investment.

Insurance

The third part of your financial plan is to carefully evaluate your present and future insurance protection. Don't overlook your insurance underwriter as a key person to have on your financial planning team. Insurance plans can be designed to suit your individual needs.

1. Life insurance. As you establish and revise your financial plan, it is important to review your life insurance policies periodically. Initially, you probably purchased life insurance to protect your family should anything happen to the primary provider, or to either you or your spouse if you are co-providers for your family.

If you are middle-aged, your children are grown, your house mortgage is paid up, and/or you have financial resources in addition to Social Security, you may wonder whether you need to continue to carry life insurance coverage at all. If this is your situation, you will want to determine what coverage you have and how it may be better used to meet your retirement needs. You may be able to convert your life insurance into a more useful vehicle.

There are a number of life insurance conversion options available. You may be able to drop part of the coverage, convert a cash value policy to term insurance, and free up some of the assets to invest. You will want to meet with your insurance agent to see what options are available to you and to determine whether or not it would be in your best interest to change your life insurance program.

If your assets are limited, regardless of your age, you may question whether you should carry life insurance at all. One consideration to keep in mind is the matter of funeral expenses. If the cost of your funeral will drain all of your cash assets, or even require your survivors to bear the expense, you may want to consider having an insurance policy large enough to protect your assets and survivors and to cover the funeral expenses.

As you review your life insurance policies periodically, you will also want to review your beneficiaries. Are the persons to whom the money will be paid upon your death the persons you want to receive the proceeds? Whoever is named as the beneficiary or beneficiaries on your life insurance policy will receive the proceeds. You have the right to change the beneficiary designation on your life insurance policy at any time you so desire—this may be particularly important to you when there is a change in your family, such as a birth, death, or divorce. The insured policy holder may change beneficiaries by completing a change of beneficiary form, which may be obtained from the life insurance company.

Trends in life insurance have changed over the past ten years. And there may be more changes in the future that could be of great benefit to you and your survivors. Recent experimental policies in Canada involve life insurance plans that pay "living benefits" directly to you should you contract a terminal illness.

Stay informed and keep in contact with a trusted insurance agent. Be sure to consult your team advisors before purchasing any insurance policy.

2. *Supplemental health insurance.* As you plan for retirement, you will need to consider future medical costs and how you will pay for them. Do you have adequate health insurance coverage, or do you need to supplement your present health insurance? As you assess your future health insurance needs, you will want to consider those needs which are not covered by Medicare.

Most older Americans have some form of health insurance or protection in addition to Medicare. Many individuals purchase private supplemental insurance known as "medigap" policies. As the name implies, medigap is designed to fill the gaps in the Medicare program. Medigap insurance policies reduce an individual's out-of-pocket medical expenses. Because of high health care costs, it may be to your benefit to purchase medigap insurance coverage. (However, individuals eligible for Medicaid, a government welfare program, do not need Medicare supplemental insurance.)

As a result of the Medicare Catastrophic Coverage Act of 1988, insurers are not allowed to duplicate Medicare coverage. Consequently, the insured will not be paying premiums for unnecessary "extra" medical coverage.

Before you purchase a medigap policy, consider the following:

- Conditions of renewability
- Selection criteria
- Whether premiums are at a fixed or flexible rate
- The company's record of paying claims
- The "loss ratio"—how much the company pays out in benefits compared to how much it collects in premiums

As you consider purchasing medigap, be sure to study the gaps in Medicare and assess your ability to pay out-of-pocket for these expenses. Be well-informed before making a decision to make sure the policy meets your needs.

3. *Long-term care insurance.* You will want to be sure you don't overlook your future health insurance needs, particularly long-term care. Long-term care refers to the day-by-day help you would need if you develop a chronic illness or long-term disability. It includes both home health care and nursing home care. Long-term care insurance is designed to cover medical expenses which are not covered by Medicare (see chapter 5), Medicare supplement insurance (medigap), or the health insurance you have through your employer.[1]

However, no long-term care insurance policy provides coverage for all expenses and most policies do not adjust for inflation. Furthermore, policies have restrictions concerning nursing home facilities and guidelines for home health care services. There are eligibility requirements you must meet in order to purchase long-term care insurance, including your age, your present health status, and the nature of any illness you may have.

Before you purchase long-term care insurance, you will

want to assess your future need for long-term care—which may be difficult to determine. Your family's medical history may provide helpful insights. You will want to consider what kinds of resources you will have available to meet your health needs and cover long-term medical expenses. Do you have savings or investments, life insurance, a pension, or a retirement plan which would help to pay these medical expenses? Do you have friends or relatives who would be able to help you either financially or even help care for you in your home?

Before you buy any type of insurance, be sure to carefully read the policies and compare the various products on the market. Don't hesitate to ask your insurance agent questions if there is something you do not understand.

Here's what to look for when comparing policies:

- How many different levels of care are offered?
- Is home health care included?
- Is there an inflation rider?
- Is previous hospitalization required?
- How many days of hospitalization are covered?
- Will your medical history be examined before you are approved for coverage?

For additional information on long-term care and nursing home care insurance, contact the Health Insurance Association of America or the National Association of State Units on Aging (see addresses on pages 163 and 176).

2
Estate Planning: What Do I Need to Do?

The first step in estate planning is to consummate your will. One of the main reasons for a will is to ensure that your estate will be distributed according to your wishes. If you have minor children, it is important that you establish guardianship for your children through your will.

If you have not completed your will, you should do so. Because a will is a legal document, it should be prepared by an attorney who is familiar with the laws of your state or province. By doing so, you can ensure that your wishes will be carried out.

If you are a widow or widower, you may need to revise or amend your will. You may not need to completely rewrite your will to accomplish this. A simple codicil (an instrument amending your will) may be enough, but it should be done in consultation with your attorney.

Estate planning issues are important for the well-being of the survivors. Dying intestate (without a will) may result in serious complications in the settling of your estate and may cause unnecessary duress for your survivors. A will helps your survivors deal with their bereavement as well as handle the additional responsibilities placed upon them in settling your estate.

Choosing an Executor

If an executor is not named in a will, most courts are likely to name a surviving spouse or close relative. It is a good idea to name an executor and an alternate executor, particularly if you have someone whom you feel would be qualified to act on your behalf. If you are an executor (personal representative) for someone's estate or would like more information about the duties of an executor, see the charts in appendix D, pages 151-2.

Although it is important to place your will or codicil in a safe place, you may not want to place it in a safe-deposit box as this may delay your wishes from being carried out. In some jurisdictions the safe-deposit box contents of the deceased are frozen, and your survivors will need to have proper authorization to have the assets and valuable papers released. At death the box often cannot be opened until an authorized person (usually the personal representative as recognized by the probate court) can arrange to meet with an official of the bank and inventory the contents of the box. Even if the surviving spouse has a key to the safe-deposit box, they may not be allowed to open the box without proper authorization.

Therefore, you may wish to purchase a fireproof lockbox in which to place your signed will or codicil. Be sure to inform your survivors where the lockbox and keys are located.

The Cost of a Will

A will is usually well worth its cost, when you consider the peace of mind you receive in knowing your estate will be distributed according to your wishes, that guardians of your choice have been established for your minor children, and that an executor you have carefully selected will settle your estate.

If you are concerned about the cost of preparing a will, there are a number of things you can do beforehand to keep the cost down. Some of these are:

1. Discuss your wishes for the distribution of your estate with your spouse and family members, and write down your decisions.

2. Select your executor and alternate executor and ask the persons you have selected if they would accept the responsibility.

3. Complete your personal and financial information forms (see appendix A, pages 137-48).

4. Make an appointment with your attorney and arrive early for your appointment. As attorneys generally base their fees on an hourly rate, you won't want to be late.

5. Take your records book, personal and financial information forms and your papers with the information regarding your decisions concerning the distribution of your estate with you to the attorney's office.

For those who cannot afford an attorney's standard fee for preparing a will, many communities have legal aid and legal services offices which provide free services to those who qualify. Check your telephone directory for a "legal aid" or "legal services" listing. If there is no listing in your area, contact your local Agency on Aging, Human Services, or Social Security or Social Insurance office as they may be able to refer you to an appropriate organization.

A Holographic Will

A holographic (handwritten) will is considered valid only in a few states and provinces and it may be contested easier than one drafted by an attorney. By relying on this type of will, you risk invalidation. If you are considering a holographic will, you will want to check the laws of your state or province to determine whether they are allowed. To ensure that your wishes will be carried out according to your stated instructions, it is vital that you have a valid will—one that cannot be easily contested or invalidated by the laws of your state or province.

Beneficiaries

Every estate plan is different because every family's situation is unique. Although there may be similarities from estate to estate such as the type and size of estate assets, each family has unique needs. These needs are based on a number of factors including age, health, and mental or physical ability of each family member. There are survivors and beneficiaries in every age group and circumstance imaginable. This is why it is so important to have an estate plan that is tailored to meet your family's needs.

Because your estate plan will have an impact on the lives of your survivors, you will want to carefully consider whom to include and how much you wish to leave as an inheritance to each of your loved ones. You should prayerfully make these decisions in your own heart and mind, and then you may want to express your desires to your loved ones. Whether or not you inform them of the inheritance they are to receive will depend upon your individual situation and *their* personalities and habits.

Other Estate Planning Tools

There are a number of other tools you can use, in addition to your will, in managing and distributing your estate. Some of these are:

Trusts

Many people ask whether there is any way to transfer assets to beneficiaries without going through the probate process. Probate can cause delay in transferring assets from a decedent's estate to the beneficiaries, and can add extra cost to settling the estate. One excellent way to transfer assets while avoiding probate is through a trust.

A trust is an arrangement whereby an individual places all or part of his assets in the management of a trustee. There are basically two types of trusts: *living trusts*, created during your lifetime, and *testamentary trusts*, which take effect after your death. Trusts may also be revocable (cancelable) or irrevocable (not cancelable). There are tax advantages to irrevocable trusts, if the remainder beneficiary is a charitable organization. The type of trust appropriate for you will depend upon the size of your estate and the tax implications.

Life Estates

With a life estate, you retain the control of your property (for example, the right to live in your house during your lifetime), but at death the property is transferred to the beneficiary named in the deed. Life estates may be revocable or irrevocable.

Outright Gifts

You can give some or all of your estate away as an outright gift while you are still living. Outright gifts may be given to individuals or an organization. Advantages of giving an outright gift may include: reduction in estate size (and therefore minimizing of estate taxes), personal satisfaction of making a gift during one's lifetime, and benefits to single persons who cannot take advantage of the marital deduction to reduce estate taxes. Lifetime charitable gifts may also result in income tax savings.

Life Insurance

You can transfer some of your wealth through life insurance which can be paid to your beneficiaries either in a lump sum or in payments over a period of time. With careful planning, life insurance can be excluded from your taxable estate.

Joint Ownership

Another way to distribute your estate is through joint ownership. There are four kinds of joint ownership:

1. *Community property.* In some states (not all), anything acquired by one spouse during their marriage belongs equally to both of them.

2. *Joint tenancy with right of survivorship.* When two or more persons own property jointly and if one person dies, their interest ordinarily passes to the other joint tenant(s) without going through probate.

3. *Tenancy by the entirety.* This form of joint ownership is generally limited to spouses. Upon the death of one spouse, the other becomes the sole owner.

4. *Tenancy in common.* Each person owns an undivided

fractional part of the property. Unlike joint tenancies, the spouse's interest is generally not included in the deceased's estate for federal tax purposes. Instead the deceased spouse's interest passes to the heirs through probate.

Deferred Giving

If you would like to leave a legacy to your loved ones and to charitable organizations in the form of a gift, you may want to consider one of the following:

Survivorship gift annuity. A gift annuity is a wonderful way to provide for the needs of your survivors, and for them to remember you after you are gone. With a gift annuity, your spouse, sisters, brothers, children, grandchildren, friends, or others—receive income for their lifetimes. Upon death of the last income beneficiary, the remainder would go to a charitable organization.

Will. You can provide for your survivors and charitable organizations by giving them a gift through your will.

Revocable trust. You can make provision for your survivors and for charitable causes you believe in through a revocable trust agreement which may pay income to your survivors.

Charitable remainder trusts. You can provide for them through either a charitable remainder annuity trust or unitrust. These may provide substantial tax advantages plus a good income.

Taxes

Many people question whether it is right to pay taxes. When the disciples asked Jesus whether it was right to pay taxes, he replied, "Give to Caesar (the government leader) what is Caesar's, and to God what is God's" (Matthew 22:21).

Taxes do impact us tremendously these days. Good estate planning considers the impact that taxes have in accomplishing your personal goals and in settling your estate. Currently, there are no estate or succession taxes in Canada. In the United States, however, estate, gift, and inheritance tax implications must be considered. These are the three basic taxes which may have an impact on the settling of your estate:

Federal Estate Tax *(U.S. Only)*

Estate tax is the tax imposed by the federal government (and some states) on the privilege of *transfering* property, *not* on the property itself.[1] It is assessed on the total value of the *taxable* estate transferred upon the person's death, "other property" which the decedent owned at one time over which he had certain rights, and taxable gifts made by the decedent after December 31, 1976.[2] Estate taxes are calculated on the basis of the market value of the assets minus allowable deductions.

Typical estate deductions include: funeral costs; administrative expenses of the estate; mortgages, debts, and liens against the estate; charitable donations; marital deduction (no tax paid if the entire estate is left to the surviving spouse); and state and local taxes. Your survivors will want to check with your accountant and financial advisors to see which estate deductions may apply as they settle your estate.

Gift Tax *(U.S. Only)*

For federal purposes, a gift tax is imposed on transfers of assets made during an individual's lifetime. It is the equivalent of the federal estate tax imposed on transfers after death. There are annual exclusions for lifetime gifts. (Some states also impose a gift tax.)

State Inheritance and Estate Taxes *(U.S. Only)*

Inheritance or estate taxes are imposed by most states. Inheritance tax is based on the relationship between the decedent and the beneficiary and is imposed upon the privilege of *receiving* property from the decedent at the time of death. State estate tax is calculated similarly to federal estate tax and may be imposed on the taxable estates of their residents, or on real and tangible personal property located within their borders whether owned by a resident or nonresident. State estate tax may be in addition to state inheritance tax.

Payment of Taxes

According to the law, each person is entitled to specify in his will which of his assets shall be used to pay the estate tax. If this is not specified in the will or a person dies intestate (without a will), the state or federal government will decide which assets will be used to pay the taxes required. Federal and state laws require that the executor (personal representative) pay taxes from the estate assets prior to distributing any of the property to the beneficiaries in the will.

Estate Tax Deductions

The following estate tax deductions are available to many estates:[3]

1. Funeral expenses allowable by the laws of the state. This includes expenses for opening the grave, monument, mausoleum, burial lot, perpetual care/maintenance, and transportation. Even when Social Security death benefits are paid to the surviving spouse, allowable funeral expenses as a tax deduction are not reduced.

2. Administration expenses allowable by the laws of the state. This includes expenses related to settling the estate and transferring the property to the beneficiaries or trustee— expenses such as executor's commissions, attorney's and accountant's fees, court costs, and so forth.

3. Claims against the estate. This applies only to those claims which represent the personal obligations of the decedent at the time of death. This includes income taxes, mortgages on property, and alimony among other things.

4. Losses incurred during the settlement of the estate. This applies to losses resulting from fires, storms and other disasters, and theft (if not reimbursed by insurance).

5. Charitable deductions. This applies to the transfer of property or assets to any state or to a charitable organization.

6. Marital deductions. The marital deduction (currently unlimited) applies when assets are transferred at death to the surviving spouse. There are special provisions for unlimited non-taxable living gifts made between spouses.

You should discuss estate, gift, and inheritance taxes with your attorney, accountant, or financial advisors who can assist you in arranging your financial affairs in order to minimize the amount of taxes you will have to pay.

Filing Tax Returns

Only those estates with assets exceeding certain minimums are required to file a federal estate tax return. As to when the estate tax return must be filed, check the instructions to the Estate Tax Return (Form 706) which may be obtained free of charge from any Internal Revenue Service office or your public library.

Filing requirement information and forms for state inheritance and estate taxes may be obtained from your state tax commission office.

Taking Care of the Basics

Perhaps you wonder if there is anything you can do now to prepare your future survivors to manage and settle your estate. There are a number of things you can do now to prepare your survivors for their responsibilities later. Some of these areas are:

Household Management

You can help your survivors by explaining your household/maintenance responsibilities to them. If there are certain tasks for which you are primarily responsible, make sure your survivors know how to perform these duties. This may include auto repairs, lawn care, household maintenance, cleaning, laundry, plumbing, heating and appliance repairs, and any other task which you have taken care of for your household. Show them where your circuit breaker box is and how to operate it. Help them learn about basic car maintenance and the name of a reliable garage.

You can help to alleviate many future frustrations by informing your survivors where your tools are located, how to handle simple repairs such as leaking faucets and squeaky doors, or how to shut off the main water supply in case of an emergency. Although your survivors may not become experts in these areas, it will be helpful to them if they at least know how to take care of the basics.

If you are responsible for most of the household chores such as cleaning, laundry, and cooking, you can help your survivors by informing them where the cleaning supplies are kept, how to use the washer and dryer including the amount of soap and bleach, the correct temperature for various types of clothes, as well as how to sort the clothes. They should know how to prepare simple meals.

Your survivors will find it helpful to know the utility and general household operating costs. Costs for normal housekeeping duties may seem astronomical for surviving spouses who have not previously handled the household budget. You will be of tremendous help to your survivors by making sure they are well-informed about your part of the household management.

Joint Bank Accounts

If you have a joint bank account with your spouse, both of you should be familiar with the account so that either spouse can take charge upon the death of the other, or in case one spouse should become incapacitated or incompetent. You should be familiar with the location of the bank statements and cancelled checks, savings passbooks, and so on. Both of you should know the account number, be able to balance the checkbook, and complete transfer and deposit slips in order to make transactions. If you are currently handling these responsibilities, encourage your spouse to take over the job for a period of time until he or she is comfortable with the procedure. Your spouse will then be prepared to assume full responsibility for these tasks upon your death.

Debts

Often, a husband or wife does not want to discuss their debts with one another. Upon death, the other spouse is left without knowing what debts have accumulated, or the amount, and to whom they are due. When bills start coming in, the widowed spouse undergoes a great deal of stress trying to sort them out. The more your spouse knows in advance, the better they will be able to cope when the time comes. It is helpful if you and your spouse both understand the details concerning your financial plan.

Avoiding Con Artists

Although there are many professionals who can be of great assistance as you plan your estate, you should be aware that there are some who would take advantage of you. There are many people (including some stockbrokers, attorneys, insurance agents, accountants, real estate agents, and others) who make their living by taking advantage of survivors in a vulnerable position. These people are con artists. Sometimes even a family member or relative may take advantage of the other survivors.

You may receive telephone calls from people who have seen the obituary in the newspaper. In order to identify how reputable the prospective advisor is, you may want to ask yourself the following questions:

1. What would he gain?
2. What would I gain?

3. What would I stand to lose? Are there any risks involved?
4. Would I have contacted this person? Did my loved one work with this person?
5. I like his ideas. Is there anyone else who could help me? If so, seek the advice of other professionals in the same field—get a second opinion.
6. Will his offer still be available in the months and years to come? Or is this a "one-time" offer? Be careful about one-time, short-term, or "get-rich-quick" offers. If anyone tries to push you into an investment decision, you should probably look for another advisor.
7. Will he agree to meet with my trusted and knowledgeable friend who can objectively evaluate his suggestions and report back to me?
8. Will he agree to meet with my trusted attorney or accountant? If so, set up an appointment. If not, you should probably look for another advisor.
9. Is he indeed employed by the company he claims to represent? You may wish to check with the company.
10. What do I know about his company? Is it reputable? You may want to check with your local Better Business Bureau or local bar association. Their addresses and telephone numbers should be in your local directory. If you cannot find the address and telephone number of a local bureau, you may wish to write or call the Council of Better Business Bureaus (United States) or the National Headquarters for Canadian Bureaus (Canada) (see addresses and telephone numbers on page 164). If you can't find the address and telephone number of a local bar association, you can write or call the American or Canadian Bar Association (see addresses and telephone numbers on page 164).

Protect Your Survivors From Con Artists

The best way to protect your survivors from being taken advantage of by a con artist is to draw up a plan in advance that your survivors can use. Instead of leaving the decision-making to your survivors at a time when they are least prepared to do so, you will have already made most of the major decisions yourself. This is one advantage of estate planning. When you do not have an estate plan, any plan may look good. Estate planning helps protect your survivors' financial security and gives you peace of mind knowing that your affairs are in order and that you have provided for your loved ones.

3
Funeral Planning: Where Do I Begin?

If the idea of making plans for your own funeral is a sensitive subject for you, you are not alone. Many people refuse to even discuss it, not to mention make specific plans and decisions.

There is something you can do that may help you with what may seem like an unpleasant task. Try to change your focus. During this time, it is natural to center your thoughts on your own death. Instead, try to see this act of planning as a tender gift to your loved ones at a time they will need it most.

When no prearranged funeral plans have been made, the survivors are faced with an overwhelming number of choices and decisions—most of which are final and need to be made immediately. All this takes place during a time of great emotional stress and vulnerability, which by its very nature makes any decision difficult. It is especially overwhelming if the key survivor has not had the experience of making funeral arrangements before.

As difficult as it may be for you to make these choices, it may be easier than having your loved ones make them. If you are married, perhaps you and your spouse can make both of your plans together. This may seem unpleasant, but many widows and widowers have found great comfort in knowing the arrangements were as their spouse had wanted. Perhaps when the two of you have finished making your plans, you could go out for a special dinner or other event to celebrate your *life* together.

Making your own funeral plans may be difficult, but try to focus on it as a gift of love to your survivors.

You may wonder where to begin as you consider how to settle your personal affairs. There are many decisions to make when planning a funeral. By making your own arrangements your survivors will know exactly what should be done when the time comes. In fact, you will already have most of the work out of the way.

Pre-Need Plans

Prearrangement is the planning of funeral services before they are needed, often years before death occurs. Prearranged ("pre-need") plans for funeral services and merchandise are being marketed more and more by the funeral industry. In fact, it is becoming a popular trend. Prepayment is not required for a prearranged funeral. There are advantages and disadvantages to these plans which you should consider.

Advantages of Prepayment Plans Are:

- Prepayment insures that money is set aside solely for the funeral and no other purpose. Generally, funds are placed in a trust or similar plan where they will accrue interest which will help to offset the effects of inflation. In most cases, the trust is revocable. Therefore, the funds may be withdrawn by the trustor at any time. At the time of death, the funds are paid to the funeral home for its services.

- Such arrangements help provide peace of mind to those who do not have a reliable friend or relative to handle their funeral arrangements and payment for services rendered.

- They also relieve family members from a possible financial burden later while under stress of bereavement.

- If your prepayment funeral plan is with a Golden Rule funeral home, there will be no change in cost no matter how far in the future death occurs. This provides assurance that no additional costs will arise for which the family or estate will be held responsible. The Golden Rule provides one of the largest and most complete full-time staffs of any association for funeral directors in the world. For more information regarding Golden Rule funeral homes in your area, contact International Order of the Golden Rule (see address on page 165).

- Moving to a new location may not be a problem. If the funeral arrangements are made with a Golden Rule funeral home, they will be honored by all other Golden Rule homes anywhere in the United States and Canada.

- If you are receiving Medical Assistance (Medicaid) or Supplemental Security Income (SSI), you can legally "shelter" assets in a prepaid funeral contract and continue to receive assistance as long as you continue to meet the government eligibility requirements.

Disadvantages of Prepayment Plans Are:

- With some funeral homes, prepayment may not cover later cost increases due to inflation. Therefore, less expensive merchandise and services may be substituted, or your survivors may be asked to cover the additional cost of providing the same quality merchandise and service you selected.

• Laws covering prepayment plans vary from state to state. Therefore, complications may arise should you move to another state, particularly if the funeral home is not a member of the Golden Rule. Should the funeral home go out of business, some contracts become null and void. This is especially true if the funeral home is an independent home.

• Regulations also vary regarding who receives the interest on the account and who must pay taxes on that interest. In some cases, funds may be removed from the account to cover administration costs incurred by the funeral establishment. There may also be restrictions on revocable plans regarding whether the prepayment is refundable in part or in full.

• Complications may result when payment is made in installments and payment is not completed prior to death in which case the contract may not be honored.

Alternatives to Prepayment Plans

There are alternatives to prepayment plans available. Instead of prepaying for your funeral arrangements, you may wish to consider one of the following options:

• Plan your funeral services through a memorial society (see page 52).

• Establish an interest-bearing account dedicated to funeral costs, such as a Totten Trust or a Savings Account Trust, with a bank, credit union, or other savings institution. A Totten Trust or Savings Account Trust is simply a savings account to which you add the name of the beneficiary. The beneficiary can be a funeral director, friend, or relative who is trusted to use the funds as you direct for your funeral expenses.

The advantage of a Totten Trust or Savings Account Trust is that the funds stay in your control should you move or need to withdraw any of the funds in case of an emergency. It is revocable during your lifetime but generally becomes irrevocable at the time of death.

- Establish a Purple Cross plan, in which the proceeds in cash may be designated to any beneficiary you name or to any funeral establishment. The Purple Cross plan is cash value life insurance on which you pay a premium for a designated period of time, or a single premium, and the face value of the policy grows yearly after that to meet future funeral needs and to offset inflation. Any amount of insurance proceeds in excess of funeral and burial or cremation costs reverts to your estate.

A funeral director would be able to refer you to a licensed insurance representative qualified to write Purple Cross Plan policies.[1]

Funerals can be partially or fully pre-funded. For more information about pre-funding your funeral, you should contact your local funeral director who would have the forms and information you would need. Should you wish to consider a prepayment funeral plan, you will want to ask your funeral director to fully explain the contract so that you understand every detail. You will want to ask him what would happen to your contract should certain situations arise.

Memorial Societies

In view of the high cost of funerals these days, you may wish to consider the services a memorial society can offer. Memorial societies are non-profit, democratic organizations with unpaid directors and officers who form a Board of Trustees elected from the membership. (These organizations are not affiliated with memorial garden cemeteries.)

Memorial societies encourage their members to plan ahead for a moderate-cost, dignified, and simplified funeral. Members believe that money spent on elaborate funerals could be better spent elsewhere, particularly for the needs of the living.

To become a member of a memorial society is relatively inexpensive. There is a one-time membership fee to be paid; however, there are no monthly or annual renewal fees or dues. Some societies may impose a "records charge" for processing the final records at the time of death. Membership is not based on an individual's income. Therefore, people with a high income as well as those with a low income may join.

Upon becoming a member of a memorial society, you receive a prearrangement form which you complete. This simple form allows you to indicate your funeral wishes in regard to the disposition of your body, the type of service you would like to have, and whether you would prefer burial or cremation.

There are more than 175 societies in the United States and Canada.[2] If you wish to become a member or if you have questions about such activities in your area, contact your local society. If you join a memorial society and move to another town, your membership may be transferred to another memorial society if you so desire. If you cannot find the address of your local society in your telephone book, contact The Continental Association of Funeral and Memorial Societies in the United States or The Memorial Society Association of Canada. They would be happy to provide this information for you (see addresses on page 164).

Memorial societies have agreements with one or more funeral directors in a community who will provide a dignified, inexpensive funeral at a predetermined cost. In general, there are no restrictions regarding the type of funeral you may have. There are usually a few basic plans from which you may select. Most memorial society members prefer no embalming, no cosmetic make up, no open-casket viewing, a low-cost casket, and a simple service. Services may be held in a church, funeral chapel, crematorium or cemetery chapel, or any other suitable location.

The Continental Association of Funeral and Memorial Societies and The Memorial Society Association of Canada serve as a voice at the national level. They are active in monitoring the entire field of funeral legislation advocating consumer rights. Memorial societies are consumer-oriented and encourage members to express their own religious and philosophical views. Therefore, they have been endorsed by major religious, consumer, senior citizen, and labor organizations. Memorial societies derive their name from the fact that they encourage "living memorials" to be given in memory of the deceased, such as donations to charitable organizations, medical or scientific research, or scholarship funds.

Issues to Be Resolved

Embalming

The practice of embalming is not new, though the methods of embalming have changed down through the centuries. For example, Mark 16:1 (NASB) states: "And when the Sabbath was over, Mary Magdalene, and Mary the mother of James, and Salome, bought spices, that they might come and anoint Him [Jesus]." Their practice of anointing with spices was their method of embalming or preparing the body for permanent burial.

Many people question whether embalming is required. Embalming is usually not required, but it is usually performed. This makes it possible to delay the disposition of the body for several days. When the funeral must be delayed to allow time for family and friends to be notified and to make traveling arrangements to the funeral location, embalming becomes necessary. It also makes it possible to achieve a more pleasing final appearance if there is to be a viewal, which may be important to the survivors.

Every person should be persuaded in his own mind whether to be embalmed or cremated. You usually have the right to choose a disposition such as direct cremation or immediate burial if you do not want embalming. A funeral with a viewal may make embalming a practical necessity and, thus, a required expense.

Cremation

Because of the high cost associated today with embalming and burial, and limited space in cemeteries, cremation has become very common. Cremation is the rapid disposal of the body by intense heat, reducing the body to ash. People often question whether the practice of cremation is biblical.

Concerning cremation, *Unger's Bible Dictionary* states:

Interment in Bible times followed soon after death, as is evident in the narratives of the burial of Sarah (Genesis 23:1-20), Rachel (Genesis 35:19-20), and Rebekah's nurse (Genesis 35:8). The Hebrews did not normally cremate, except in most unusual cases of emergency, as in the case of Saul and his sons (1 Samuel 31:11-13)....Later Babylonians burned their dead and deposited their ashes in ornate funerary urns, as did Greeks and Romans. Hebrews in later time, indicated by the numerous ossuaries found in New Testament Palestine, also practiced cremation.[3]

Organ Donation

Many people receive satisfaction knowing that by donating their organs they will be helping others. By donating your body or organs, you may save another's life after your death.

Medical schools accept donation of the body for research purposes. This may be whole-body or organ donation. With whole-body donation, there are minimal costs involved in regard to disposition of the body as the medical school may transport the body at little or no cost to you. The Uniform Anatomical Gift Act allows for the donation of the body or specific body parts or organs upon the death of the donor. If you desire to donate your body to a medical school, you should preregister with your nearest school.

If you choose to become an organ donor, you can still have an open-casket funeral, if you so desire, as there is no disfigurement or delay in funeral services. Organs can be donated by completing a donor form such as one from The Living Bank (see address on page 167). The Living Bank is the only national multi-organ donor registry in the United States. It is not a medical or storage facility. Once you have completed the donor form and returned it to The Living Bank, you will receive a donor card which you should carry with you at all times. Upon notification of a member's death, The Living Bank refers the case to the regional organ procurement agency to carry out the donor's wishes. It is in the discretion of the medical professionals to determine which donated organs are medically acceptable for transplant.

If you would like to donate your organs to a medical/ transplant facility, or your body to a medical school, you should share your feelings with your family so that they will understand your wishes and will be prepared to carry them out when the time comes. In most cases, no organ or tissue donation will be accepted unless your family approves. The cost for removing the organs or tissue is taken care of by the transplant team. Once organs are removed, the body is the physical and financial responsibility of the family or power of attorney.

If you are interested in organ donations, you may want to contact the American Council on Transplantation or the Medic Alert Organ Donor Program (see addresses on pages 167).

Medical Decisions

Because we live in an era of amazing advances in medical technology, the issues of life and death have become a major concern for many families. In the past two decades, many families have been faced with deciding the extent to which life-support systems will be used to sustain the life of a family member. When families are forced to make this important decision without knowing that person's wishes, they are placed under a great deal of stress. They seek to do what they believe to be morally and ethically right, and what they believe their loved one would want to be done under the circumstances. It is always helpful when critical issues like these are discussed beforehand.

Making Your Own Funeral Arrangements

The Funeral Rule

In 1984, the Federal Trade Commission developed a trade regulation concerning funeral industry practices, called the Funeral Rule.[4] This regulation enables consumers to obtain information about funeral arrangements, making it easier to compare prices among funeral directors.

Funeral Expenses

There are four main categories of funeral expenses as defined by The National Funeral Director's Association:[5]

1. Funeral director and mortuary staff services. This includes use of facilities, purchase of casket and funeral merchandise selected by you or your survivors.

2. Disposition of the body. This will depend upon the method chosen whether burial, entombment, cremation, or donation. Burial indicates a grave in soil or entombment (above ground) in a mausoleum. The cost involved with burial includes a cemetery lot, the casket, burial vault or grave liner (to support the earth around and above the grave), and a fee for opening and closing the grave. The cost involved with entombment includes the price of the mausoleum crypt, whether indoor or outdoor (such as a garden crypt), and charges for opening and closing the tomb or crypt.

The costs involved with cremation may vary depending upon whether the remains will be buried, scattered, or placed in a niche in a columbarium in a cemetery. Other costs include the cost of cremation itself and the purchase of an urn if one is desired.

Your survivors should know *where* you wish to be buried, entombed, or cremated. If buried or entombed, where is the lot or crypt located? (This usually must be prepaid.) If cremated, how and where do you want the ashes disposed of? Do you want the ashes buried, entombed, or scattered? It is helpful to provide a full description of the lot or crypt location so that your survivors will know which site you had previously selected and purchased.

Provide your survivors with the name, address, and telephone number of the cemetery or crematorium as well as the name of the person you contacted. It is helpful to keep your canceled check for the lot in your records book. Your survivors will need to know whether you want a marker or inscription plaque and what you want on it. In planning your funeral, you may purchase the marker in advance. Veterans are given a marker free of charge from the government. Its use is optional. Your survivors need to know where the marker was purchased in order to have the date of death inscribed on it.

3. Memorial costs. Memorial costs include the cost of the monument or grave marker (if buried or entombed), memorial niche in a columbarium with an inscription or a plaque (if cremated), and cost for "perpetual care" to upkeep the cemetery.

4. Cash advance sales. Cash advance items are goods or services that are paid by the funeral director on your behalf. These costs may include: honorariums to clergy, organist, and soloist (optional); limousines, police or motorcycle escort; flowers; obituary notices in newspapers; and various other costs which may be incurred, including certified copies of the death certificate. The Funeral Rule requires funeral providers to inform you in writing if they charge a fee for buying cash advance items. Most funeral directors charge you their cost for these items while others add a service fee to their cost.

Purchasing Funeral Items

When arranging a funeral, you can purchase individual items or buy an entire package of goods and services. As a consumer, it may be helpful to have an itemized list of the costs. When funeral arrangements are completed, your funeral director will complete a Funeral Purchase Agreement (also known as a Statement of Funeral Goods and Services Selected, see sample in appendix F, page 157) which gives an itemized summary of the charges for the services you selected. "Good faith estimates" are given for those costs which are not known at the time of arrangements, such as transportation between cities. Let's look at each of the itemized funeral costs in more detail.[6]

Itemized Funeral Costs

Basic service charge. This is the fee for the funeral director's services which may include: cost of maintaining facilities and staff, administrative details such as filing the death certificates and claims for death benefits, and placing death notices in newspapers. The more your survivors do themselves, the more the overall cost of the funeral will be reduced.

Transportation. This fee involves the transporting of the body to the funeral home or mortuary from the place of death.

Embalming charges. If the deceased is embalmed, there will be a fee for the embalming procedure which may be listed separately or it may be included in the basic service charge from the funeral home.

Body preparation. There is a charge for the preparation of the deceased, which includes washing of the body, cosmetology, hairstyling, manicuring, dressing the body, and placing the body in the casket. This fee may be omitted if the deceased is cremated or there is no viewal at the funeral or memorial service.

Casket prices. There are four basic types of caskets: cloth-covered wood, finished hardwood, metal, and sealer-type metal. Each has its own advantages. Prices will vary depending upon the type of casket selected. A pine casket is the least expensive. The middle price-range wooden caskets are covered with copper or bronze. The high price-range caskets may be constructed from mahogany or another fine-quality wood. These caskets may be covered with copper or bronze. There is no law regulating that a body which is to be cremated must be placed in a casket.

Burial vault. Most cemeteries require the use of a burial vault or grave liner to support the earth above and around the grave. Prices vary depending on the type of material and the functions it provides (such as waterproofing).

Facility charges. When the funeral service is held in the chapel at the mortuary, there will be a charge. Other optional items offered include: acknowledgment and prayer cards, memorial folders, thank you cards, guest register, and charges for the visitation or the viewing room.

Vehicles. There will be a charge for the hearse, limousines for family members and pallbearers or other participants, and motorcycle escort.

Miscellaneous costs. There may be miscellaneous costs incurred such as: death certificate filing, death notices in newspapers, flowers, honorariums for clergy and others, garments which may be purchased from the mortuary, and other services that are available.

The Funeral or Memorial Service

Planning your own funeral or memorial service provides an opportunity to make the service more meaningful and personal for your survivors. It also insures you that your personal feelings will be honored. Most people feel strongly about some funeral customs, but few put their feelings in writing.

There are many decisions you can make regarding the service. You can put as much time and thought into it (and as much heart) as you desire. This is especially helpful if your survivors do not live nearby and don't know your friends and personal preferences. The following are things either you or your survivors will be asked to decide:

Viewal. Do you wish to have visitation (viewal) at the funeral home? This is usually held the day before the funeral. Do you wish to have viewal prior to the funeral service? Or would you prefer a closed-casket service?

Military honors. If you are a veteran with an honorable discharge, or an active-duty service personnel, you are entitled to a graveside service with full military honors including a flag for the casket, a gun salute, and the playing of "Taps." There are many options as to how this may be done. You may wish to contact your local Veterans Administration office.

Type of service. Religious, civil, or other.

Graveside service. Do you wish to have a short interment service at the grave site after the memorial service?

Location and clergy. Where would you like the funeral to be held? Who would you like to officiate?

Pallbearers and honorary pallbearers. It is customary to select six friends or relatives (usually men) to serve as pallbearers. You may also choose to select six others who are given the title "honorary pallbearers." This is helpful when there are friends or relatives you would like to select as pallbearers, but perhaps they are unable to serve because of their age or physical handicap.

Music. Are there people in particular whom you would like to play the organ or piano, or have as soloists? Are there songs or hymns that are personal favorites? Or, are there any you would prefer *not* be used?

Verses and readings. Do you have special Scripture verses that are meaningful to you, or that would offer comfort to your survivors? Are there favorite poems or passages from a book you'd like read or printed in the bulletin? Whom would you like to do the reading?

Message. Is there a special theme you'd like the clergy to emphasize? Are there any words of comfort or a testimony you would like shared with your survivors? Anecdotes about your life are a wonderful way to make the service warm and comforting for your survivors—especially an anecdote on the lighter side. It's good for people to laugh or smile during a funeral. It may help relieve tension.

Eulogy. Writing a brief history of your life including family, hobbies, accomplishments, and dreams is helpful. It can be used to help write the notice for the newspapers and can be included in the service.

Luncheon. Some churches will ask if the family would like a meal or luncheon to be served after the service. There may be a charge, especially if it is a large funeral.

Marker. What would you like engraved on your marker or plaque? Do you want your full name or a nickname used? Do you have a favorite Scripture verse or a quote you would like included?

Memorials. You may also wish to designate how and where you would like money to be given as memorial gifts in your memory.

As a guide for making your own funeral arrangements, see the Funeral Planning Worksheet and Cemetery Decisions (appendix E, pages 155-6).

For information which your survivors may use as a guide in carrying out your funeral arrangements, see our Funeral Checklist (appendix E, pages 153-4). For additional information on funeral planning, see the list of resources on pages 164-7.

Part II
Surviving a Loss

4
Coping With Death: What Should I Do First?

It is almost certain that at some point in your lifetime you will be responsible for making the arrangements for the funeral of a loved one. Most people have no concept of how many decisions they will be asked to make—especially during the days prior to the funeral. If no preparation or pre-planning was done, the survivors are left with an overwhelming number of choices to make and things to do. And all of this is required of them at possibly the most stressful and painful time of their life.

Perhaps you have lost a loved one now, or are expecting it to happen in the near future. My heart and my prayers go out to you. Perhaps I can offer some comfort, and help make your journey ahead a little easier, by providing a list of most of the decisions you will be expected to make. By its nature death upsets the order of your life. Having an organized approach to the responsibilities you will face may help by giving you a sense of order—and by guiding you through this next stage in your life. It may help you remember to do the important things at a time when you are faced with so many new responsibilities.

Survivors' Tasks Before the Funeral

These next pages will help "walk you through" the process of making or carrying out the funeral arrangements. In appendices E and F, on pages 153-8, there are forms and checklists in greater detail to help you keep track of the decisions you make in an orderly manner.

Notification

The first step you need to take after the death of a loved one is to notify the family, friends, and people who will be helping you make the necessary arrangements.

First, if they haven't already been involved, contact a doctor and the funeral director. You may also want to contact your pastor or clergy at this time. They too will have many preparations to make and will want to meet with you as soon as they are able.

Next, make a list of immediate family, friends, and relatives who will need to be contacted. A list is helpful to keep track of who has been called and who hasn't. You may want to ask one or two people to help make the calls. Include calling *your* closest friends. In the confusion, this is often overlooked. Your close friends will want to know what has happened so they may offer help and support.

Then you will want to contact the deceased's employer and business associates.

Preparation

As soon as possible, you will want to locate the following papers of the deceased:

1. Pre-need funeral documents (if any)
2. Birth certificate

3. Social Security number
4. Military discharge papers (if applicable)
5. Marriage certificate (if applicable)
6. Organ donor card
7. Visa or citizenship papers (if applicable)

Body Disposition

The funeral or memorial society director, or medical research institution will need to be called for removal of the body. Often your doctor will offer to make this call for you. You will need to inform them of the kind of disposition: burial, cremation, or donation of body to a medical institution.

The Coroner and the Medical Examiner

When a coroner's investigation reveals the need to employ scientific methods to determine the cause of death, the body is brought to the county morgue where it is held until an autopsy can be performed. Homicides, suicides, and accidents come under the coroner's or medical examiner's jurisdiction. Autopsies may be performed at the request of a physician with the family's consent. Most hospitals have pathology departments which process the information pertaining to the autopsies performed at their hospital.

The Death Certificate

The death certificate is concise summary of the pertinent data describing the deceased and the cause (the means by which the person died, such as a heart attack), mode (natural, accidental, suicidal, homicidal), and place of death. (In Canada, proof of death can be established by a death certificate, attending physician's statement, or a Funeral Director's Statement of Death.) The death certificate is signed by the physician and/or the medical examiner or coroner, local county registrar, and the mortician or funeral director. A death certificate is a legal document (see sample in appendix G, page 159) which affects the distribution of property, life insurance and other death benefits, and payment of pension, and Social Security benefits (see chapter 5).

The survivor(s) need to obtain eight to ten certified copies of the death certificate for use in filing claims. A certified death certificate is embossed with the state/county seal. Death certificates are usually filed with the county court administration and the state department of health.

A valuable resource is a booklet entitled, "Where to Write for Vital Records" (DDHS Publication No. [PHS]87-1142). It is available from the Public Documents Distribution Center (see address on page 174).

Funeral Director Arrangements

When the funeral director is notified of the death, he will want to make an appointment to meet with you as soon as possible to start making the arrangements. Some of the first things he will ask you to do are:

1. Provide personal information (and possible obituary information) (appendix A, pages 144-6)
2. Funeral goods: casket, vault, etc. (appendix F, page 157)
3. Provide clothing and personal items for the deceased (appendix E, page 155)
4. Decide on location of funeral, burial site (or other), flowers, funeral service details (appendix E, pages 155-6)
5. Cemetery decisions (appendix E, page 155)
6. Pallbearers (appendix E, page 155)

Funeral or Memorial Service

Your pastor or clergy will need to know how involved you want to be in the planning of the service, or if the deceased left instructions or personal wishes. Some of the types of things they may ask are:

1. Kind of service: religious, military, civil
2. Music, musicians, and organist
3. Scripture, prayer, special readings
4. Graveside service
5. After service luncheon or gathering

Cemetery or Crematorium

1. Purchase lot, crypt, and vault (if not prearranged)
2. Make arrangements for burial (grave opening and closing), entombment (opening and closing), or cremation (instructions for remains)

Other Duties

The property of the deceased should become an immediate concern. If they owned their own home or lived in an apartment, ask a neighbor or friend to keep a close watch on the property. Unfortunately, burglars also read the obituary columns.

If the deceased was living in a nursing home or long-term care facility, be sure to ask how soon their personal property must be removed. Some facilities allow as little as twenty-four hours.

Keep a record of memorials given in your loved one's honor. Some will be designated to be used in specific ways and others may be used as the family desires. Save sympathy cards and records of memorials for later acknowledgment.

Survivors' Tasks After the Funeral

Even though the majority of the decisions will have been made prior to the funeral, there will still be many responsibilities after the service. These will also be important, but you will have more time to consider them. These responsibilities may include:

1. Arrange for disposition of flowers
2. Send notes to acknowledge memorials and expressions of sympathy
3. Meet with attorney to begin probate proceedings
4. Determine what death benefits (Social Security, life insurance, veterans' benefits, pension) are available to you as a survivor and file claims with appropriate agencies.

Probate

Probate is the legal procedure by which the court accepts or rejects a document as being the will of the deceased. It is the process by which an estate is settled and the property distributed. When the validity of the will is proved, an executor is approved or appointed, estate matters are carried out, and property is distributed to the beneficiaries. The period of probate includes time for interested persons to contest the validity of the will, if they so desire. Probate may take just a few months or over a year depending upon the size of the estate and the circumstances involved. During this time, notices to creditors are published in the newspapers so that outstanding claims against the estate can be paid.

When there is a will, one must follow the probate process so that the deceased's property shall pass to those named in the will. This process may vary from state to state or province to province. However, most states have a printed form generally entitled "Petition for Probate" which must be filed with the appropriate court in order to begin the probate process.[1] In Canada, application for "Letters Probate" must be filed with a court of competent jurisdiction, generally the surrogate court.[2]

Usually the executor (personal representative) named in the will submits the Petition for Probate or application for Letters Probate. However, the petition could be submitted by the surviving spouse or an adult child. In general, any interested person can submit the petition or application. The court, petitioner, or applicant may send notice of petition to the interested persons (usually those named in the will who have a direct and immediate financial interest in establishing the validity of the will). Once the court approves the petition, an order is issued to accept the document as being the deceased's will and to appoint a personal representative for the estate if one is not designated in the will or if the person has died intestate (without a will).

In Canada, Letters Probate certifies that the will has been approved and registered in the court. The grant of Letters Probate is evidence that the will is valid. If the person dies testate, the court issues "Letters Testamentary" which grants the executor the authority to handle the affairs of the estate. If the person dies intestate, the court will appoint an administrator by granting the administrator "Letters of Administration" which gives the administrator the right to handle the property of the deceased.[3] Usually a spouse or close relative is appointed as administrator. However, it is in the sole discretion of the court, and the court may decide to appoint a trust company should the closest living relative be unwilling or unable to accept the Letters of Administration.

It is vital that you have a will to avoid unnecessary delay or added expense in the probate process. In Canada, there is a shorter waiting period for Letters Probate (when the person dies testate) than for Letters of Administration (when the person dies intestate). [4] Provincial statutes may prescribe that the beneficiaries be responsible for the debts of the deceased for up to one year from the death of the person who has died intestate.[5]

The purpose of probate is fourfold: 1) to establish owner-ship of the property and to transfer ownership of the prop-erty to the person or persons entitled to receive it, 2) to ensure that those who are entitled to receive the property actually do receive it as directed in the will, 3) to file the deceased's terminal tax returns and tax returns for prior years due but not yet filed at the time of death, to prepare and file the estate income tax return, and 4) to obtain tax releases or clearance certificates from the Internal Revenue Service (United States) and Revenue Canada (Canada) prior to distributing the estate to beneficiaries[6] and, in the United States, to pay federal and state death taxes (estate and inheritance taxes) that are due from the estate.[7]

How Others Can Help

If you are a friend, relative, or neighbor of someone who has lost a loved one in the past few years, there are a number of things you can do to express your love and concern for them.[8]

1. **Answer the telephone** at the home of the bereaved for the first day or two. Later, your telephone calls, especially at lonely times, would be appreciated.

2. **Take them for outings** at times when they may be feeling especially lonely, such as on holidays, birth-days, and anniversaries.

3. **Home security** is a particular concern to the wid-owed. Offer to stay with the bereaved person for a period of time until he or she is able to adjust to an empty house. A widow or widower would appreci-ate the installation of deadbolt locks on the doors, if needed. Check the windows to make sure they lock

securely. It is wise to have someone house-sit at the time of the funeral. Burglars read the obituaries too!

4. **Talk** about the loved one. Don't be afraid to mention his or her name.

5. **Listen intently** and encourage the survivors to talk about their loved one and to express their emotions honestly. This is probably the single most important thing you can do to help someone work through the grieving process.

6. **Have realistic expectations** as you understand that the grieving process takes a long time.

7. **Show concern and genuine care,** but not pity.

8. **Treat the survivors** as human beings who are intelligent and capable, not as though they are fragile or incompetent.

9. **Express your own emotion** with the survivors. If you feel like crying, do so. It may help the survivors to cry with you. This is better than trying to avoid the pain or pretend it doesn't exist.

10. **Say nothing** rather than offering cliches or pat answers. A hug or holding the person's hand often means more than mere words.

11. **Pray** for and with the survivors. This may be of great encouragement as you ask the Holy Spirit to comfort those who mourn.

12. **Bring food** or take them out for dinner. It may be hard for them to prepare meals, especially if they have lost their appetite.

13. **Walk** with them. It is good to walk and talk, and exercise (in moderation) will help the survivors have more energy at a time when it is needed most.

14. **Provide transportation.** Do not allow the survivors to drive for the first week. They may feel confused, and even in familiar surroundings they will need concentration to drive.

15. **Give a gift** in memory of the deceased. Memorial checks are often preferred to cash gifts, and eliminate any confusion in recording and acknowledging the gift. Gifts made to a tax-exempt, charitable organization are tax deductible.

16. **Write notes and send sympathy cards** to the survivors. When you write a note, share your own memories and emotions rather than to quote Scripture or write a "sermon." Allow the Holy Spirit to use you to minister to the bereaved.

Concerning the Widowed

The Bible tells us to "rejoice with those who rejoice; mourn with those who mourn" (Romans 12:15). If we have parents, grandparents, aunts and uncles, brothers and sisters, or other relatives who are widowed, we have a responsibility to God to care for them. Paul writes, "Give the people these instructions, too, so that no one may be open to blame. If anyone does not provide for his relatives, and especially for his immediate family, he has denied the faith and is worse than an unbeliever" (1 Timothy 5:7-8). It is vital that the church consider how to meet the needs of the seniors, not all of which are monetary needs. Our church has started a program called "Senior Saints" which focuses on the needs of seniors in the church by planning social/fellowship activities. Through this program people of all ages can minister to the seniors and be ministered by them in return.

The senior widows or widowers are responsible to God for the way they treat others. Paul instructs the senior widow to be "well-known for her good deeds, showing hospitality" (1 Timothy 5:10). Even though they are in need themselves, the widowed should continue to do what they can to help others who are in need as well. They should show others the same type of kindness they have received.

Each person's grieving experience is different. As a senior widow, you may have been raised to believe that your self-worth is based on your roles as a mother and a wife. Upon the death of your husband, your grief may be intensified by the loss of your self-image. If so, you will need to re-evaluate the basis for your self-image. As you become more involved in the community and your church, you may find a new basis for your self-image. Remember that ultimately our self-worth comes from the Lord's evaluation of us and not our own.

The church should recognize that there may be some young widows or widowers who would need to receive support from the church either on a short-term basis or perhaps for a longer period of time. These young survivors should not be overlooked. Our church has an elder's fund (contributions given by the members of our church) for the express purpose of helping families who are in need. We also have a food shelf and clothing drive. These are just a few ways we can help to meet the needs of others.

Widows in the Church

How then can we seek to meet the needs of those in the church who are widowed and in need? You may wish to consider a number of ways you could meet the needs of the widowed in your local congregation. Just as the needs are many and varied, so are the opportunities for meeting those needs. You may want to form a committee and list as many ideas as you can and then determine which ideas could be implemented by your church.

We received a letter from a dear woman named Sylvia, in North Carolina, concerning one idea her church has developed to meet the needs of the single or widowed in their congregation. Her pastor visited a widow after Christmas. When he asked the woman whether she had a nice Christmas, she replied, "I stayed home all by myself."

Because of this experience Sylvia's pastor implemented an "Adopt a Friend" campaign in his church so that those who are single or widowed would be remembered not only on holidays but other times during the year as well. He wrote names, addresses, and birthdays of every single or widowed person on cards for the congregation to select. It has become a tradition at Sylvia's church to adopt a friend each January and to remember them throughout the year.

The first year Sylvia adopted an aunt. She then adopted an uncle and another aunt who have both since passed away. Sylvia has visited her adopted aunts and uncles many times over the years. What is amazing is that Sylvia has shown Christian love to her adopted aunts and uncles while she herself has epilepsy and is disabled. She has experienced a great deal of physical pain, having undergone numerous operations, and understands the emotional pain many single and widowed people experience due to loneliness.

Sylvia writes, "I never could give up their names. The very first aunt I adopted, I still have. I love her so much, and I tell her so. I have the very first card she wrote to thank me for having her at my house for lunch after church one Sunday. She includes me in all things. My aunt has had two heart attacks. I went to the hospital to visit her, and when I was in the hospital, she sent me flowers."

Even though Sylvia is now confined to her home due to health problems, she continues to minister to those in need. She calls people who are sick or lonely to encourage them. In memory of her mother, she has flowers placed in church on Mother's Day. She also had flowers placed in the church on Mother's Day for her adopted aunt to take home after the service.

May Sylvia's prayer echo in our hearts, "God, make me a blessing to your glory." Jesus Christ loved us so much that he went to the cross. I owe not part of myself but all of myself to God. If we believe in the Lord Jesus Christ, we shall be saved. We are never alone no matter how we might feel.

5
Survivors' Benefits: How Do I File Claims?

A survivor is very busy during the first few months after the death of a loved one, with many forms to complete and problems to face. There are a number of survivors' benefits which may be available to you. While survivors' benefits cannot ease the difficulty or take away the sorrow caused by death, they can ease some of the financial burden. You should not feel guilty when filing claims for survivors' benefits. Your loved one would want your financial needs to be met.

Survivors' benefits may include: Social Security, veterans' benefits, life insurance, health insurance, Medicare, employer and trade union benefits, and IRAs. If you are eligible to receive any of these benefits, you must file a claim. Benefits will not be automatically sent to you, even if the agencies have been notified by the funeral director—unless he filed the claim on your behalf. The sooner a claim is filed the sooner the benefits will be paid.

There are a number of important papers and documents regarding the deceased which you may need to present to the agencies in order to file claims for survivors' benefits. Before you file any claims, gather the information you will need (see appendix A, page 141 for a list of important documents).

Social Security Benefits

Social Security benefits are available to qualified applicants. They can be paid to the spouse or family of a deceased worker. These benefits can help to ease the financial burden a family may feel after the worker's death by providing the family with a continuing source of cash income.

Social Security benefits may be paid to the following survivors:[1]

1. Widow or widower age sixty or older

2. Widow or widower age fifty or older who is disabled not later than seven years after the worker's death

3. Widow or widower who has a child under age sixteen or a child disabled before age twenty-two

4. Unmarried child under age eighteen

5. Unmarried child disabled before age twenty-two

6. Divorced spouse (a) caring for a child under sixteen or a disabled child, (b) age fifty and disabled, (c) age sixty and was married to the worker for ten years. Remarriage after age sixty (age fifty if disabled) will not prevent the payment of benefits.

7. Grandchildren, great-grandchildren, and dependent parents age sixty-two or older may qualify

Filing Claims for Social Security Benefits

You can apply for survivors' benefits at any Social Security office. You should file a claim as soon as possible after the worker's death.[2] The people at the Social Security office will need certain information to complete your application. You can provide this information from the important documents which you have gathered.

You will also need to provide evidence of your relationship to the deceased to prove that you are eligible to receive Social Security survivors' benefits. This evidence may include your marriage license (if you are the spouse) or birth certificate and proof of financial support if you are a dependent. For a list of information you may need to provide, see appendix H, page 160.

Payment of Social Security Benefits

When you go into the Social Security office, you should bring your checkbook or savings passbook so they can arrange to have your checks deposited directly into your account. Direct deposit is safer and more convenient for you and more efficient and economical for the government.[3] If you do not have a bank account or do not want your checks deposited directly into your bank account, your checks can be mailed to you. It may take three months or longer before you start receiving benefits.

For more information about survivors' Social Security benefits, call your local Social Security office. You can find the address and phone number of the nearest office in your telephone book under "Social Security Administration" or "U.S. Government," or write or call Social Security Administration headquarters (see address and phone number on page 168).

Veterans' Survivors' Benefits

Certain benefits are available to eligible survivors of deceased veterans of wartime or peacetime service who were discharged under conditions other than dishonorable. If eligible, these benefits may include income to the spouse and children.

Types of Veterans' Survivors' Benefits

Dependency and indemnity compensation. DIC payments are authorized for surviving spouses, unmarried children under age eighteen, and certain parents of deceased service personnel or veterans.[4]

Death compensation. Death compensation payments are authorized for surviving spouses, unmarried children under age eighteen, and certain dependent parents of deceased veterans.[5]

Death pension. Certain surviving spouses and children of deceased eligible veterans may qualify for non-service connected pensions. Surviving spouses and unmarried children under age eighteen of deceased veterans with wartime service may be eligible for pension based on need if they meet the applicable income standards.[6]

Survivors and dependents' education. Survivors of deceased veterans and children between eighteen and twenty-six years old are eligible to receive benefits when the veteran's death was the result of service in the armed forces.[7]

Medical care for dependents of survivors. The Civilian Health and Medical Program of the VA (CHAMPVA) is a medical benefits program through which the VA helps pay for medical services and supplies received through civilian services by eligible dependents and survivors of certain veterans.[8]

Death gratuity. Death gratuities are paid to surviving spouses and dependents when death occurs during active service, or within 120 days from causes related to active service. This is paid as soon as possible after death. If not received within a reasonable amount of time, inquiry should be made to the service branch concerned.[9]

GI loans. A veteran's surviving spouse who has not remarried is eligible for GI loans to acquire a home if the veteran died as a result of service connected disabilities.[10]

GI insurance. Some veterans may have carried Servicemen's Group Life Insurance (SGLI) or Veterans' Group Life Insurance (VGLI).[11] Designated beneficiaries may submit their claims to:

Office of Servicemen's Group Life Insurance
213 Washington Street
Newark, NJ 07102

Veterans Funeral Benefits

Death benefits are available to assist with the burial and funeral expenses of veterans and certain dependents of veterans.[12] Assistance for burial of dependents and survivors is limited to interment in a national cemetery. Detailed information regarding eligibility and interments is contained in the VA pamphlet, *Interments in National Cemeteries.* Copies may be obtained from any VA office which will provide information and assistance in filing burial request applications (see address for Veterans Administration on page 168).

Burial request applications should be filed only at the time of the veteran's or eligible dependent's death by contacting the Director of the National Cemetery where burial is desired. Certain funeral benefits are available in Canada.

For more information, write to the Department of Veterans Affairs (see address on page 168).

Filing Claims for Veterans' Survivors' Benefits

If you are a survivor of a deceased veteran or active duty service personnel, contact the nearest VA regional office or state veterans assistance office to file a claim. You will want to file your claim as soon as possible after the death to avoid any delay in receiving the survivors' benefits. Be sure you have the necessary papers with you at the time you file your claim(s). (See appendix H, page 160.)

A booklet available through the Veterans Administration offers complete information regarding veterans' benefits. Call your local VA office and request the IS-1 Fact Sheet entitled, "Federal Benefits for Veterans and Dependents" or write to the Veterans Administration (see address on page 168).

Life Insurance Benefits

Your insurance agent or agency should be able to assist you in completing the necessary forms to file a claim. You may wish to call the insurance company and contact the claims department. Before you meet with your insurance agent, gather the important documents listed in appendix A, page 141, as you will need some of this information in order to file a claim for benefits.

Specifically, you will need a certified copy of the death certificate as proof of death, the birth certificate of the deceased, proof of your identity and relationship to the deceased (your birth certificate and marriage license), claim forms (which you may obtain from the insurance company), and the insurance policy. In cases where death occurred under special circumstances (for example, accidental in which case accidental death benefits may be payable depending upon the policy), you may be required to complete other forms as well.

You may wish to contact the insurance company directly should the agent not have claim forms on hand or should he no longer be employed by the same company. You may wish to request that the claim forms be sent to you directly rather than to the agent. This may facilitate the claims process should the agent not be available at the time the forms arrive.

Eligibility to Receive Life Insurance Benefits

In most cases there is one beneficiary who is eligible to receive life insurance benefits. However, there may also be contingent beneficiaries who would be eligible to receive benefits should the primary beneficiary no longer qualify either due to death or other special circumstances.

In order to determine who is eligible to receive life insurance benefits, it is best to check the life insurance policy. Policies are only issued to those who have an insurable interest in the person on whose life the policy is taken out. In certain cases, a trustee may be eligible to receive death benefits from a life insurance policy. However, this could only occur if the trustee was named as the beneficiary of the policy.

Ineligibility to Receive Life Insurance Benefits

There may be some special conditions in which a beneficiary would not be eligible to receive life insurance benefits. In most cases where the insured person's death was the result of suicide (in the first two years after the policy is taken out), the beneficiary would not be eligible to receive death benefits from the life insurance policy. However, you may wish to check the policy to make sure.

A beneficiary would not be entitled to receive death benefits from the life insurance policy if the insured person's death was due to an undisclosed illness at the time the policy was taken out. This is referred to as the "contestability or incontestability clause" in the life insurance policy.

Payment of Life Insurance Benefits

Life insurance benefits do not go through the probate process if they are paid to a named beneficiary. As beneficiary, you should receive your checks within one to two months after the claim is filed unless there are complications regarding your claim. Life insurance can be paid in a lump sum or in a series of installments. At the time you file the claim, you select the payment option you wish. You may choose to have the checks direct deposited into your bank account if you so desire. Your insurance agent or agency would be able to answer any questions you may have regarding your claim.

Disputes Regarding Claims

The state Commissioners of Insurance in the United States or provincial Superintendents of Insurance in Canada can be relied upon to mediate if there are any questions or disputes regarding your claim (see addresses on page 168-9).

Special Circumstances Regarding
Life Insurance Claims

If the insurance company or agency with whom you had taken out the policy is no longer in business, you should contact your state Commissioner of Insurance (United States) or provincial Superintendent of Insurance (Canada). They should be able to provide you with the name and address of the insurance company whom you should contact regarding the validity of your claim. If the insurance company is no longer in business, it doesn't necessarily mean that the policy is valueless. It may be that the insurance company has been consolidated with another larger insurance company in which case the policy may still be in force.

If you do not know the name of the insurance company, or if the policy is missing, you can contact the American Council of Life Insurance (ACLI) (see address on page 163) and request a form entitled, "Information for Missing Policy Inquiry." After you have completed and returned the form, ACLI will forward your form to insurance companies who will review their records. If a missing policy is found they will contact the beneficiaries directly.

Health Insurance Coverage

If you are a widow or widower and were previously covered under your spouse's health insurance plan, contact your health insurance company (or your spouse's employer if you were insured under a group health plan) to ask whether you and your dependent children are still covered. Health insurance companies allow a grace period during which time the survivors are able to establish their own health coverage, so that you are not left without health coverage immediately following the death of the primary insured person. Be sure to find out how long the grace period is for your policy.

Medicare

Medicare is the federal health insurance policy for people sixty-five or older and certain disabled people. It is administered by the Health Care Financing Administration of the U.S. Department of Health and Human Services. Social Security Administration offices across the country take applications for Medicare and provide general information about the program.

Generally, if you are sixty-five and sign up to receive Social Security, you will be enrolled in Medicare. If you decide to delay receiving your Social Security benefit (perhaps because you continue to work full time), you may still elect to sign up for Medicare. People who are under sixty-five and disabled may also be eligible for Medicare. If you are not eligible for Social Security, you can buy Medicare coverage by signing up during the three months before you reach sixty-five or during open enrollment periods. Spouses must apply separately for coverage.

There are two parts to the Medicare program: Part A (hospital insurance) and Part B (medical insurance). Hospital insurance helps pay for inpatient hospital care, medically necessary inpatient care in a skilled nursing facility after a hospital stay, hospice care, and some home health care. Medical insurance helps pay for doctors' office visits, outpatient hospital care, ambulance services, and other necessary medical expenses.

Medicare does not cover custodial care that is not reasonable and necessary, and other services such as routine physicals, dental care, drugs and medicines purchased without a doctor's prescription, eyeglasses, and hearing aids.

Claims can be submitted when someone who had Medicare dies. If the bill was paid by the patient or with funds from the patient's estate, reimbursement will be made to the executor of the estate or to a surviving family member of the patient's immediate family.

If the bill has not been paid, payment can be made by Medicare directly to the doctor or medical facility or to the executor of the estate who has the legal obligation to pay all debts due by the deceased.

All beneficiaries of the Medicare program receive the

Medicare Handbook, which gives detailed information about the Medicare program. If you would like a copy of this handbook or information on Medicare benefits, contact the Health Care Financing Administration (see address on page 169) or any Social Security office.

Employer and Trade Union Benefits

Write a formal letter to your loved one's employer, union, professional organizations, or any other group with which he was affiliated. Inform them of the death and ask for any information about group life and health insurance policies, annual leave or sick pay due to your loved one, special funds, pensions, or other benefits which he may have been entitled to receive. There may be a number of benefits that you will be entitled to receive as his survivor. It may be helpful to have a friend or relative write these letters or make the telephone calls for you.

Financial Decisions

IRAs

If your spouse had established an Individual Retirement Account (IRA) and you are the survivor beneficiary, you may be eligible to start receiving benefits from the account. You will want to contact the bank, savings institution, or mutual fund with which your spouse had established the IRA. Notify them of your spouse's death and request information concerning the survivor beneficiary's eligibility to receive benefits. You may be required to furnish information from the important documents you have gathered and complete forms in order to receive benefits.

Budgeting

There are three basic steps you can follow as you begin to determine your financial needs. First, take an inventory of your present assets including savings and investments. You may want to include one or more of the financial professionals in this process. They will be able to assist you in compiling a list of the type and value of the assets in the estate.

Second, determine your annual income. Include: salary if you work, your survivor's benefits and other benefits, as well as other assets which produce income.

Third, determine your income needs. Establish a budget based on your income and expenses. Be sure to include all means by which you receive an income (see worksheet in appendix I, page 161). Leave a margin in your budget for unexpected expenses or emergencies. Review your checkbook stubs or cancelled checks for the past year(s) to determine past income and expenses (see worksheet in appendix I, page 161). This will help you to evaluate what your future income needs will be.

Once you have established your budget, you are ready to determine how your inheritance and survivor's benefits should be spent or invested. If you start spending your inheritance and survivor's benefits before you establish your budget, you risk squandering the money which could have been wisely invested had you done your planning first.

Investments

As a survivor, you will need to decide how to spend your inheritance and survivor's benefits. However, you should be aware that it may be particularly easy to lapse into spendthrift habits at this time. Survivors often purchase new items after the loss of their loved ones. Some are necessary purchases; others may not be. Be careful if you find yourself buying items with little or no thought given beforehand.

Many survivors become accustomed to writing large checks to pay for the funeral expenses (if not prepaid) and other items. It may be easy to simply continue writing checks for large amounts. Before you realize what has happened, you may end up spending your entire inheritance and savings in ways you wouldn't have otherwise.

If you need financial advice regarding how to invest your inheritance and what survivors' benefits may be available to you, you should consult a certified financial planner (CFP) and a certified public accountant (CPA) who can answer your questions concerning investments and taxes.

Making an investment requires careful planning. Therefore, you should gather the information you need prior to making investment decisions. In this way, you will be better equipped to design a safe, long-term financial plan. It may be in your best interest not to concern yourself with making investment decisions right after the death of your loved one.

Credit Cards

Upon death, advise creditors to cancel at once all credit cards belonging to the deceased. You may wish to have the creditors issue new credit cards in your own name.

Exercise caution in the use of credit cards. Excessive use of credit cards can easily lead to debt and even bankruptcy. Your spending plan should depend upon your family's needs as well as your values and beliefs.

Automobile Title and Licensing

If you inherit an automobile you must have the title and license registration changed to your name. You will want to write to the licensing and title division in your state or province, as each state or province has different laws governing this procedure. Whenever inquiries are made in writing, it is a good idea to keep a copy for future reference. If the car title is still held by a bank, the person who inherits the vehicle will also be responsible for paying off any unpaid portion of the contract.

Utility and Household Accounts

Place a call to the gas, electric, telephone and other utility companies to have the name on the account changed. Often widows want to leave the telephone directory listing in their husband's name. This can be done even though she uses her own name as the person to be billed. It's also possible to have your initials, rather than first name, listed in the telephone directory.

Young Survivors With Dependent Children

If you are a young survivor with dependent children, one of your primary concerns is the care of your children, including the finances required to meet their present and future needs. You will want to consider how to best use the inheritance and survivor's benefits you receive to provide food, clothing, and shelter for your children and how to invest for their future which may include their education and other goals.

If the money you have inherited is absolutely necessary to provide for your children's present needs, you shouldn't worry about saving for the future. Nevertheless, you should consider setting aside a sum of money—even if it is a small sum—regularly to save for your children's future as well as for your retirement. A small sum consistently set aside will add up to a substantial amount over a period of years. "Dishonest money dwindles away, but he who gathers money little by little makes it grow" (Proverbs 13:11). You may want to consider the options available to you for earning additional income, and be sure that you haven't overlooked any benefits which are rightfully yours or your children's. Be sure to file for the survivors' benefits you or your children are entitled to receive.

Young Survivors Without Children

Although you may not have the responsibility to meet the needs of children, you do need to consider how to best use your inheritance to meet your own present and future needs. You will want to be particularly careful not to lapse into spendthrift habits—which may be easy to do at this time. You could wind up completely exhausting your inheritance and depleting your savings.

Middle-Aged Survivors

If you are a middle-aged survivor whose children are grown and on their own or you do not have any children, you may not know how you would like to spend your inheritance, and there may be a number of options available to you. These may vary from going on vacation to giving the inheritance to your children or grandchildren or saving it for your retirement (which may mean an early retirement). Whatever your options, you will want to carefully consider how to best use your inheritance to accomplish your goals and fulfill your heart's desires. Because there may be a number of options available, you will want to allow ample time to carefully consider each option before you make your decision.

You will need to consider present and future medical expenses including home care, nursing home care, and hospital costs. You will want to consider whether purchasing long-term care insurance would be beneficial in light of your circumstances and your family's medical history (see chapter 1, pages 29-30).

Senior Survivors

If you are a senior survivor on a fixed income, you may need to use the inheritance you receive for your living and medical expenses. If you are a senior survivor with an adequate or substantial income, you may have other options available to you. You may desire to use your inheritance to support those causes you firmly believe in. From such an "investment," you will reap eternal rewards.

Many people derive deep satisfaction from giving gifts to their loved ones. "A good man leaves an inheritance for his children's children..." (Proverbs 13:22). Through his Word, God declares the kind of sacrifices that are acceptable to him—sacrifices regarding how we should treat those who are poor and destitute in society as well as our own family members. Isaiah 58:7 (TLB) reads, "I want you to share your food with the hungry and bring right into your own homes those who are helpless, poor and destitute. Clothe those who are cold and don't hide from relatives who need your help."

When we are under stress, we tend to make decisions we would not have made otherwise. With the concerns you may have regarding things like investments and wills, there may be times when you will feel uncertain about your future. Making your decisions slowly and carefully will help you regain a sense of security.

6
Housing Options: Should I Move?

Decisions, Decisions, Decisions

The decisions of Americans about their lifestyles, where and in what kind of homes they will live, are shaped by a broad spectrum of changing forces. Traditionally, personal health and family ties have had a major, if not predominant, role in such decisions. Recently, concerns about inflation, increased costs in property maintenance, and taxes have forced more and more survivors, particularly widows and widowers who live alone, to make decisions about where they live and what kind of housing they choose or more accurately, where they can afford to live.[1]

There is no single solution to the housing needs of those who are now facing life on their own. This is because people have various interests, needs, and goals. There is a valuable resource available to assist you in determining your housing needs. It is a workbook entitled *Your Home, Your Choice*, published by the American Association of Retired Persons in cooperation with the Federal Trade Commission (see address on page 175).

Housing decisions are often based on the loss of a spouse and family ties. Family ties work in two directions. On the one hand, there is the desire to move closer to the children and other relatives at a time of bereavement. This is a particularly powerful force for the newly widowed. Many have found it easier and more comforting to live with family or friends at this difficult time. If family and friends are close, there is often no desire to consider relocating.

On the other hand, it is clear that family ties impose an inhibiting force if a person desires to relocate. In any case, you should be careful not to be pushed into a decision which you may regret later. You may want to consider whether moving away from or closer to family members and friends would help ease your bereavement or simply cause you more difficulty depending upon your individual situation.

Many people contemplate basic changes in their living arrangements, location, and lifestyle activities when they are left alone. If you are a widow or widower, one of the most important decisions you will need to make is in regard to your housing situation. Whether to remain in your family home, or in the same community, is a very personal choice which only you can make. There can be a lot of unhappiness involved if moves are not made carefully and prayerfully. As a widow or widower, it may be best not to make this decision too soon after your spouse's death as locational moves have an almost certain finality. In order to make the decision that is right for you, you will want to carefully consider your reasons for moving and the housing options that are available to you.

To Move or Not to Move

When considering the question of staying where you are currently living or relocating, there are a number of factors involved. Important aspects to be considered may include:[2]

Medical facilities. It is important to consider whether you will have ready access to doctors, hospitals, and other medical services.

Transportation. You will want to consider the availability of public transportation, particularly busses. Is public transportation available to take you where you want to go—church, shopping malls, grocery stores, restaurants, doctor and dentist, parks, concerts?

Climate. Weather may be a determining factor in your decision to move to a new location. Cost may be a factor in connection with climate especially if you will need to pay for heat and air conditioning.

Recreation. What kind of leisure activities are available? This may be another determining factor particularly if you want to be active in clubs, social activities, and community events.

Pets. If you own or would like to own a pet, you will want to consider whether pets are allowed or whether there are any restrictions concerning the type of pet you may own.

Children. If you would like to have your grandchildren come for an extended visit, you will want to consider whether children are allowed and what the restrictions might be regarding the length of stay for children and other visitors.

Employment or volunteer opportunities. If you would like to seek employment or volunteer your services, you will want to consider what opportunities are available.

You may wish to use the Housing Checklist (see appendix J, page 162) as you determine how each of these factors affects your decision.

Staying Where You Are

There are some strong reasons for staying where you are:[3] (1) expenses of your present home are already part of your budget which you expect to be able to meet in the future, or if you rent, you don't expect the rent to increase substantially; (2) you would like to avoid the trouble and expense of relocating; (3) you would remain near family, friends, and neighbors where you are familiar with the community; (4) your present home fits your needs, and it is neither too big nor too small; (5) you enjoy the climate; (6) your present community offers adequate facilities for medical care and other services; (7) there will probably not be any major community deterioration to reduce property values.

Keeping Your Own Home

The first option is to stay in the home that you already own. The home you own can often provide a relatively low-cost roof over your head. This is especially true if the mortgage is paid. Many families have insurance to cover the payment of a home mortgage if the head of household dies. This means that your principal costs are now upkeep and property taxes. If a spouse, particularly the head of a household, dies at a fairly early age, it is usually best for the surviving partner to remain in the family home. Often there are children and a move to another location only adds to the trauma of death and separation. If you are happy in your home, have an excellent church fellowship, enjoy family and friends close to you, it may be best to stay where you are.

Home ownership offers an important advantage over renting. You cannot turn in rent receipts for cash, but you can always sell a property if, for some unexpected reason, you need the money. Well-located housing is expected to continue rising in value. Should you need cash and not want to sell your home, you may want to consider these options:

1. Housesharing. Consider having someone live with you—for example, a college student or other single person. This is commonly referred to as "housesharing," and usually involves two or more unrelated people living together in a house, large apartment, or other type of housing. Each person normally has some private space (usually a bedroom) while sharing common areas such as the kitchen, living room, dining room, and the yard. This type of arrangement has economical and social advantages. By sharing housing and utility bills, you will reduce your own costs. With another person in the house, you will have someone to talk with, to share meals with, to help with the household chores, to provide protection and increase security, as well as to provide assistance in case of an emergency. For more information about shared housing programs, contact the National Shared Housing Resource Center (see address on page 170).

2. Conserve energy. You can do this by shutting off rooms or entire floors to save on heat, air conditioning, and upkeep costs.

3. Rental apartment. Turn part of your home into a rental apartment. Be sure to check zoning regulations and estimate remodeling costs involved beforehand.

4. Start your own business. You may wish to use part of your home to run your own small business: sewing/alterations, small appliance repairs, income tax preparation, etc. Again, be sure to check local zoning laws and restrictions as well as tax consequences before you start your business.

5. Home equity. There are ways to take advantage of home equity. Equity is the difference between what you owe on your house and its appraised value. For example, if the house you bought seven years ago for $75,000 is now appraised at $150,000 and you owe $30,000, your equity is

$120,000 ($150,000 − $30,000 = $120,000).

One way you can take advantage of your home equity is through home equity conversion. Home equity conversion is a program that enables the home owner to free up the equity in his home in order to purchase needed services. Some banks participate in home equity conversion programs and may be able to help you free up these resources.[4] However, home equity plans may not be available in all communities nor are they in the best interest of all homeowners. Investigate and compare home equity plans carefully and obtain the advice of your legal and financial advisors as there may be risks involved.

A primary source for more information is the National Center for Home Equity Conversion (see address on page 170). Another valuable resource is a U.S. government booklet, *Turning Home Equity Into Income for Older Homeowners*. Although this booklet is designed for retirees, it is valuable to others who want to plan for the future. It is available from the U.S. Government Printing Office (see address on page 175).

Community Services

If you prefer to stay in your own home in a familiar neighborhood, you may find that regular or even occasional help can make your life much easier. If you need assistance with housework, home maintenance and repairs, lawn care, personal care, nursing, or cooking, you may want to take advantage of community services. To discover what kinds of community services there are available in your area, you may want to contact your State Unit on Aging office.

Check your local telephone directory under "County Government" for an "Aging" listing. Because of the Older Americans Act of 1965, State Units on Aging exist in every state and U.S. territory.[5] Area Agencies On Aging address the concerns of seniors at the local level. Your local area agency should be able to provide you with a list of resources concerning the community services which would be available in your area. For more information, contact the National Council on the Aging (see address on page 173).

Non-profit organizations such as churches and senior citizens centers may offer community services as well as your local hospital and convalescent center. Although there are many community services available to seniors, not all services are available in every community. The kinds of community services most commonly available are:

1. *Home health care* provided by trained home-health aides to assist recovering, disabled, or chronically ill persons in personal care, hygiene, physical exercises, meal preparations, and light housekeeping in the home environment. Homemaker services may be available to help with daily household chores, laundry, shopping, transportation, and errands. For information on home care, contact the National Association of Home Care (see address on page 170).

2. *Adult day care* enables seniors to spend daytime hours benefiting from planned social activities.

3. *Home delivered meals* (commonly called "meals-on-wheels") provide nutritionally balanced meals to individuals in their own homes.

4. *Group dining programs* offer low-cost nutritious meals to seniors in a group setting such as a senior citizens center.

5. *Companion services* provide care and protection to seniors in their own homes on a day, evening, weekend, or live-in basis.

6. *Telephone reassurance* provides regular telephone contact to isolated seniors to ensure their continued well-being and social contact.

7. *Transportation services* are often available to seniors either on an individual or group basis to shopping malls, churches, doctors offices, etc.

8. *Senior centers* are available in many communities and offer a wide variety of social and recreational activities to seniors.

9. *Respite care* is provided by paid workers who come into the house for short periods of time or by a nursing home where a patient may go for a short stay to give family members a rest or vacation.

10. *Hospice care* for the terminally ill may be provided in the home by a hospice or a hospice service. Hospice care is designed to ease the physical and emotional suffering of the individual rather than to focus on treatment or a cure.

For additional information about what kinds of community services are available or to find out if your state has an American Association of Homes for the Aging (AAHA) affiliate, contact AAHA (see address on page 169).

Moving to a New Location

To consider a move is difficult. Most people find that their home is their friend, and they desperately want to keep it. However, if the family home is large and requires considerable maintenance, that decision becomes critical.

There are some valid reasons for moving:[6] (1) your home is now too big, too expensive, or otherwise unsuited for continued occupancy; (2) too much of your capital is tied up in your home and could provide needed income if properly invested; (3) your neighborhood has declined and may cause loss of property value or change your lifestyle. If the neighborhood is improving too rapidly, rising taxes and the cost of services could become a burden; (4) the community offers few opportunities for social, cultural, spiritual, and physical activities you now desire; (5) health and other valuable services are not available or are minimal; (6) you do not like the climate or realize it is negatively affecting your health or your doctor recommends that you move to a more suitable climate; (7) your children and many of your friends have moved. If you are a widow or widower living alone, it may be easier for you to relocate than for a widow or widower who has children at home.

Selling Your Home

The disadvantage of staying in a home that has greatly increased in value over the years is that you may not be making the best use of this asset. If you would like to sell your home, you should consider the tax consequences that may result from the sale of your home. You should give this matter careful consideration before you put your house on the market.

If you are fifty-five years of age or older, you are entitled to a one-time exemption from taxation for up to $125,000 of capital gains.[7] This means that taxes are exempt on up to $125,000 gain from the sale of your home or from the cumulative gains of homes you have sold over your lifetime and on which you have previously deferred the gain. However, you must claim this exemption—it isn't automatic.

If you sell the home and relocate, you can possibly take advantage of the one-time $125,000 capital gains exemption and put your profit to a much better use. One wise move may be to sell your present home if there is a high appreciation and buy down to a less expensive and perhaps more practical home. If you pay cash for a new home, you may have a substantial amount remaining to invest and produce income for living expenses.

In order to claim the one-time capital gains exemption, there are certain qualifications you must meet:[8]

- You or your spouse must be fifty-five years of age or older.
- The home must be your principal residence, and you must have lived in the home three of five years prior to the sale.
- It is a one-time exemption. Therefore, neither you nor your spouse can claim the exemption more than once.

As you evaluate the tax ramifications of selling your home, be sure to seek advice from your accountant or financial planner.

Renting Out Your Home

Instead of selling your home, you may wish to consider renting it to someone else. The advantage to renting your home would be the benefit of receiving rental income while retaining the option to sell your home at a later date when the value of the property may have increased. You may even wish to consider renting a portion of your home and living in the other portion yourself.

One disadvantage to renting your home may be the amount of time and energy needed for maintenance and upkeep of the property. If you are unable or do not want to take care of the property yourself, you may be able to make an arrangement with the renters to do the maintenance and upkeep for a reduction in rent. Otherwise, you would need to hire someone to do the work.

Buying a New Home

Single-Family Home

It may still be in your best interest to own your own detached, single-family house. You may not want one as large as your current residence, but you may want a yard if you enjoy gardening or lawn care. If you should decide to look for another house, you will want to consider the following:[9]

1. *Construction.* It is of vital importance how well the house is built. It is often best to hire a professional building inspector to evaluate the property. This is important if you are buying an older house or a newly constructed house which may not have warranties.

2. *Repair problems.* How old is the house? Are there items which will require immediate repair or replacement? How much will essential repairs cost? What impact does that cost have on the listing price of the house?

3. *Location.* Real estate people have often said, "The three most important features of a house are location, location, and location." There are two sides to that coin. Because your house will be an investment as well as an aesthetic living space, you will want to be sure that the area is not on the decline to avoid potential decreases in value. Conversely, you will want to avoid an area where values are rising rapidly as that will most likely signal increases in taxes and services.

4. *Utilities and taxes.* These can be the most uncontrollable costs in housing. Ask to see copies of utility and tax bills. Are there energy-savings features in the house such as storm doors and windows, insulation, cost-efficient furnace, etc.?

5. *Living space.* Look at the living space to be sure it will meet the needs you have as a single person or the needs of your remaining family. Is it the kind of home you will want to live in when your children have moved out on their own? Will your furniture fit in the new house or will you have to sell your furniture and buy new items? Will you have adequate storage space? Is the house small enough not to be a burden but large enough to accommodate you and your family's needs?[10]

Cooperative (Co-op) Purchase

If a single-family home is not your choice, you may be interested in a co-op if these are available in your area. A co-op is a situation where you do not own your individual apartment. Rather, you own a share of the entire cooperative complex or building.[11] With that ownership you have a right to occupy your specific unit or apartment. In addition to mortgage payments, you will pay a monthly fee or rent to the co-op corporation to cover your share of the building mortgage, property taxes, maintenance, and general costs. One advantage of a co-op is that there are no individual settlement fees when you purchase since the corporation already has a mortgage for the entire complex or building.

When you sell, you sell your stock. There is no deed to transfer. The cooperative is owned by its residents. You have a voice in how the cooperative is run because you are part of the management. The owners have the right to use the common facilities which may include a swimming pool, game room, exercise room, social facilities, and lounges. Co-ops may provide bus transportation and other services for residents.

One major disadvantage is that these apartments are often very expensive as the monthly fee may increase due to a rise in maintenance expenses, taxes, and other general costs. Another disadvantage is that when selling your stock other owners may veto the sale if they do not approve of your buyer. Before purchasing, check to be sure the structural conditions are safe, the operating costs and financial reserves are adequate, and the amenities offered are sufficient for the number of occupants. Before signing any contract, have a lawyer review it.

Additional information regarding co-ops is available from the National Association of Housing Cooperatives (see address on page 170).

Condominium Purchase

Another housing option is purchasing a condominium (condo). When you purchase a condo, you are purchasing a housing unit that is your own. You are buying part ownership of the common-elements which may include hallways, party rooms, and swimming pool. The owners of the condominium elect a board to manage the facility. They do this through self-management or by hiring a management organization. For these services, the owners pay a maintenance fee each month in addition to the cost of the apartment which is arranged through a financing organization. Condos come in various shapes and sizes: high-rise, low-rise garden style, or townhouses, and even unattached houses.[12]

There are some advantages to owning a condo:

1. Cost. Condos are somewhat less expensive than single-family homes since they are generally smaller, have joint walls, and require less land space. However, in most areas of the country, condos can fluctuate in price from quite economical to very expensive. This depends on location and how luxurious a lifestyle the owner desires.

2. Maintenance-free. The owners need not concern themselves about the lawn, roof repairs, or pool maintenance. The owners are released from yard work and have more time for themselves. Most condo owners are happy with the arrangement.

There are also some guidelines to be considered when looking for a condo:[13]

1. *Location.* As with any other housing purchase, location is a prime consideration. Location of a condo has a lot to do with the resale value.

2. *Construction.* It is always wise to have the facility inspected by a building inspector who is familiar with condos. One of the primary requirements is good soundproofing since the walls are shared.

3. *Fees.* Research the monthly fee you will be paying for maintenance, insurance, taxes, etc. You will want to consider how frequently the fees have been increased in the past. If you are purchasing in a new development, be especially careful of what is called, "low balling." This happens when the original developer holds fees at a low level to attract new buyers. Once he leaves the development in the hands of the owners, a sharp increase in fees is needed to meet the actual costs.

4. *Budget.* Ask for a copy of the operating budget to see if the fees are realistic. Furthermore, check to be sure the owners association has an adequate reserve for emergency repairs and unforeseen expenses.

5. *Amenities.* Elaborate club houses, tennis courts, paid social directors, olympic pools, etc. may raise the monthly fees. You will want to consider whether these amenities are of value to you.

6. *Management.* Check out the philosophy of the man-

agement group if the owners are not providing self-management through the board. Does the management firm work in cooperation with the residents? Do they listen to the concerns of the residents?

7. Hidden problems. As an example, in the early years of condo construction, the developers maintained ownership of the land or the recreational facilities. This was accomplished through ninety-nine year contracts and often allowed for sharp increases to adjust for inflation. Currently, "rec. leases" are banned by law. Nevertheless, you may want to avoid projects where those kind of escalation or ownership clauses are still in effect.

For additional information on condominiums, write for a booklet published by the U.S. Department of Housing and Urban Development. This booklet is available free from the Consumer Information Center (see address on page 174).

Manufactured Homes

Under the 1980 Housing Act, what was called the "mobile home" the government says is now to be called a "manufactured home."[14] They are factory-built homes set on permanent subdivision lots. Many look just like conventional houses. They are generally sold and financed with the lot included. The popularity of this kind of housing is growing as cost of conventional construction continues to increase. They are placed in beautiful park settings with paved streets, green lawns, driveways, sidewalks, club facilities, swimming pools, and many other features. Today's mobile/manufactured home parks represent a vast improvement over those of the earlier days of the industry.

Some concerns for study and research of manufactured homes are:[15]

1. Lot fees. In addition to the purchase of the basic home, generally you must pay monthly rent for the lot on which the dwelling is placed. These fees can range from under two hundred dollars to over several hundred dollars. These fees can, and usually do, increase.

2. Construction. Check the manufacturer carefully both for quality of construction and warranty policy. Because of construction problems in the past, a one-year warranty is required to meet federal standards. However, a continuing problem is that some builders do not honor the warranties or are slow about repairing defects. Check location of heating systems, insulation, and resistance to wind from storms.

3. Park rules. Your personal standard of living may be affected by the rules established by the park operators. One thing to check is that you do not have to move out after your home reaches a certain age.

4. Appreciation. Historically mobile homes have suffered a lack of appreciation. However, with the coming of the manufactured home, that is changing. Today, many modern mobile homes hold their value or actually appreciate if they are located in the newly developed and highly desirable parks.

5. Financing. The 1980 National Housing Act raised the maximum for Federal Housing Association (FHA) insured loans and authorized the Federal National Mortgage Association (FNMA) to create a secondary or re-sale market for mobile-home mortgages. Another advantage of the mobile or manufactured home is that in most cases it can be purchased with cash. If purchased with cash from the sale of a previous home, there may be some funds remaining which can be invested to earn income for the surviving spouse.

For further information on mobile/manufactured homes, write to the Manufactured Housing Institute (see address on page 171).

Retirement Housing

Other housing options specifically designed for retired seniors are:

Nonprofit Retirement Communities

These facilities are often sponsored by a church or other nonprofit organization and include a basic apartment, food service, medical care, and social or recreational amenities. These multipurpose facilities attempt to serve residents as their needs change. Therefore, a person who needs to move from a fully equipped housekeeping apartment to a personal life-care unit can do so with a minimum of uprooting. Life-care communities offer various levels of medical care for life. If permanent nursing care is required it can be provided in the same environment. Most of these work hard to maintain an atmosphere of wellness by separating the living quarters of the ill from the well. For more information on life-care communities contact the American Association of Homes for the Aging (see address on page 169).

Several types of arrangements are available to finance these non-profit homes. One method is the founder's fee. Under this plan the resident pays a fee and is entitled to lifetime occupancy of an apartment. Usually, based on life-expectancy tables and costs, an amount is paid for total life-care which will include accommodations, meals, health, and personal care services. Should the resident live beyond life expectancy, the sponsor must still continue care. These church-sponsored facilities are very popular, and the residents enjoy a happy living environment and lifestyle. A caution is to carefully check all aspects of the contract.

Profit Retirement Communities

Many retirement villages are self-contained developments offering single cottages, homes, or apartments to those who are newly retired and to seniors. They may provide maintenance for a monthly fee. Some retirement communities offer a clubhouse, activity programs, and health programs. There are even some retirement communities with diagnostic and treatment clinics on the premises, and many have a resident doctor or nurse.

Most retirement communities have come into existence since the mid 1950s. The population of these centers is gradually increasing as more and more people consider them to be excellent places of residence. In general, the emphasis is upon leisure living, and it appears that a subculture of leisured seniors may be emerging. Again, the caution is to be sure of the various costs and fees and the contract which is executed.

Whether you are considering a nonprofit or profit retirement community, you will want to evaluate the pros and cons of retirement community living. Pros may include: social and recreational activities, opportunity to meet other retirees; no upkeep (snow shoveling, yard work, or major repairs); a safe environment with security buildings, nursing care available; etc. Cons may include: crowded apartment complex; high cost; segregated from people of other age groups; strict rules and regulations; too many social activities, etc.[16]

In addition to considering the pros and cons, you will want to investigate the community yourself. Talk to the management and residents. Ask yourself whether you would be happy living in a retirement community.

Retirement Apartments

A fairly new housing phenomenon is currently in vogue. It is found mainly in larger cities and is called a "retirement apartment." This is becoming a choice option for senior survivors who do not want to move from their community. However, they do want to be around contemporaries and have the benefit of some services.

These apartments are available for a monthly rental fee which generally includes: the apartment itself; housekeeping services; transportation to stores, shopping centers, and banks; at least one main meal (included in the monthly rental); and a nurse or doctor on call in the event of an emergency. An advantage of this type of housing is that the resident can enjoy a lovely apartment and numerous amenities without a large investment in purchase or entry fees. There may even be extra funds from the sale of the family home which can be invested for retirement income. Be sure to read the lease carefully before signing it.

Nursing Homes

Basic Services

There are four types of basic services offered by nursing homes:[17]

1. *Nursing care* which requires the professional skills of a registered or a licensed practical nurse. Services include: administering medications, injections, physical therapy, occupational therapy, laboratory and x-ray services, dental services, etc.

2. *Personal care* which includes help in walking, getting out of bed, bathing, dressing, eating, etc.

3. *Residential services* which includes a planned program for the social and spiritual needs of the resident as well as room and board.

4. *Medical care* which includes the care of a physician who visits periodically, medication, rehabilitative procedures, special diets, and other treatments.

Levels of Care

Different nursing homes offer different levels of care. The types of nursing homes include:[18]

1. *A skilled nursing facility (SNF)* is a nursing home which provides twenty-four-hour-a-day care (registered nurses, licensed practical nurses, and nurse aides) for a person who has serious health care needs but does not require the intense level of care provided in a hospital. Rehabilitation services may also be provided. Many of these facilities are federally certified, which means they may participate in the Medicare or Medicaid programs. For more information regarding what Medicare covers, write for a free booklet, Medicare: *What It Will and Will Not Pay For*, published by The American Society of Internal Medicine (see address on page 169).

2. *An intermediate care facility (ICF)* is a nursing home which is generally federally certified in order to participate in the Medicaid program. It provides less extensive health care than an SNF. Nursing and rehabilitation services are provided in some of these facilities, but not on a twenty-four-hour-a-day basis. These homes are designed for persons who can no longer live alone but need a minimum of medical supervision or assistance and help with personal or social care.

3. Board and care (or residential care) facilities provide shelter, supervision, and care, but do not offer medical or skilled nursing services. They stress the social needs of the individual rather than the medical needs. Unlike the SNF and ICF facilities, board and care facilities are not licensed to receive reimbursement under Medicare and Medicaid programs. In some states, the residents of board and care facilities may receive financial assistance through a state supplement to the individual's Supplemental Security Income (SSI) payment.

4. Adult day care facilities provide nursing and nutritional services in a comfortable non-residential environment. Many nursing homes have adult day care programs. Adult day care enables seniors to make their own decisions while providing them with long-term care.[19]

5. Boarding houses are not nursing homes even though they have a common ancestry. Boarding houses are generally not licensed, regulated, or inspected as are nursing homes. Boarding houses generally do not provide nursing care around the clock. However, home health agencies and visiting nurses may offer individual care to those who need it. Basically, boarding houses and nursing homes are only similar in that they both have a large number of senior residents.[20]

Choosing a Nursing Home Facility

It is best to anticipate ahead of time that you may need nursing home care. It is important to participate in the decision making process whenever possible rather than to leave these decisions to your family and friends. Early planning allows time for full exploration of the options available so that you will be prepared to make the best choice at the appropriate time.

Four primary factors affecting the choice of a nursing home are: (1) the type of care required, (2) the financial resources available, (3) the convenience of location, and (4) the availability of a room. In many states, pre-admission screening is required prior to admission to a nursing home.[21]

The first consideration in selecting a nursing home is to ensure that the facility can provide the type of care needed. Questions about what care may be needed should be discussed with the physician.

The second prime factor is a frank analysis of your financial status. There should be a complete inventory of available resources. This includes: source and level of income; property; savings accounts; stocks and bonds; pension provisions; insurance, Social Security and veterans' benefits (see chapter 5), and any family assistance available.

If you cannot afford to pay for nursing home care, hospital or local social service departments will provide information about eligibility requirements and procedures for applying for assistance from publicly financed programs. If you are not able to pay for nursing home care, your choice of a nursing home may be limited to a facility which accepts Medicare or Medicaid (see definitions in Glossary) and has an opening.

The third factor is to decide on the best geographic location. A good choice is a facility which is most convenient to family and friends. The best way for families to assure quality care for a senior relative in a nursing home is by visiting the nursing home and communicating with the nursing home staff.

Another consideration is availability of rooms. Many nursing homes have waiting lists. The length of time you may be on a waiting list is relatively unpredictable. A room may become available within days, or it may take weeks or months. If you are certain you want to go to a specific home that often has a waiting list, you may want to have an alternative place planned where you could stay in the interim.

For more information regarding housing, see resource list on pages 169-71.

7
Grieving:
Is It Natural and Necessary?

"Blessed are those who mourn, for they will be comforted."
(Matthew 5:4)

The Grieving Process

Grieving is not a permanent state, but rather it is a process—a long process. It can't be rushed. Allow yourself and others time to grieve. Death may be sudden, even when expected, but you may continue to feel certain emotions resulting from your loved one's death for a long, long time.

Grieving is a natural and necessary part of life. Most people in our society today do not understand the importance of grieving. What many people fail to recognize is that grieving is a natural result from loss of a loved one and that it is necessary for the bereaved to undergo this process in order to incorporate the loss into their life experience.

Signs of Grief

If you have lost a loved one, the inclination you may feel to grieve is natural. You shouldn't feel ashamed to show signs of your grief. Crying, impulsive behavior, indecisiveness, lack of appetite, disorganized thoughts and behavior, forgetfulness, insomnia or sleepiness, and loneliness are all normal signs of grief.

I remember going to the grocery store shortly after our baby boy, Samuel, died. It was almost impossible to concentrate in order to find the items on my grocery list. I wandered up and down the aisles looking for canned vegetables. When I finally found the vegetables, I had a difficult time trying to decide which ones to buy. I even wondered if I was going crazy. Now I know that my indecisiveness was a normal part of the grieving process. I also experienced sleepiness, forgetfulness, lack of appetite, and loneliness. Some days I could hardly get motivated to do anything. For long periods of time, I would just sit and stare at our baby's picture. The death of someone close to you can shake your life right to the core.

You will find it beneficial as you go through the grieving process if you have a good friend, relative, or neighbor with whom you can openly display your emotions. It is especially helpful if you can share your feelings with someone who has also experienced grief in the past. After Samuel died, my husband, Brian and I met many couples who had also lost a child (or children) through miscarriage, stillbirth, or shortly after birth. The Lord surrounded us with people who understood and shared our sorrow. We were not alone. We are so thankful for these new friends we have met as a result of our loss.

Stages of Grief

In discussing the grieving process, it may be helpful to define three stages in the grieving process. Bereavement, the first stage, is when the survivor experiences the shock or denial of the loved one's death. Grief, the second stage, is the wide variety of emotional responses the survivor experiences which may include anger, guilt, depression, and confusion as well as other emotions. Mourning, the third stage, is incorporating the experience of loss into daily life. When the survivor begins to understand and accept the loss, he has entered the recovery (mourning) stage in the grieving process.[1]

The grieving process is different for each person. How your loved ones deal with their own grief may be very different from how you deal with yours. That's okay. Each person is unique. Therefore, how you grieve will be different from how others grieve and adjust to the loss in their lives.

Sometimes well-meaning family, friends, and neighbors may say they "know how you feel." Truthfully, they really don't. They may understand to a certain extent some of the emotions you may be experiencing, but only you know how your emotions are affecting you. This is not to say that we should not try to understand one another's grief. But we need to recognize that we cannot fully understand how another person feels.

Therefore, we should not be quick to make judgments like, "He should be over it by now. After all, it's been six months (or two years, or ten years)." There is no specific time when someone should be "over it." When we have lost someone we love, we have lost a part of ourselves. There will always be reminders that they are gone which stir the emotions of grief. These reminders may crop up six months, two years, or even ten years after their death. As time goes on, these reminders become less painful. We may even welcome them because they remind us of our loved ones and help to keep their memory alive.

Aspects of Grief

As you go through the grieving process, it may be helpful if you understand some of the specifics concerning this process. Although everyone's grieving experience is different, the following are some very common aspects of the grieving process.[2]

1. Crying. There are times when tears may be expected such as at the funeral or on a special day such as your anniversary, birthday, or a holiday. Crying is a natural part of the grieving process. Yet, you may cry at unexpected times or in unexpected places. Two weeks after our baby had died, I went into the doctor's office. The nurse knew that my visit was a postpartum check up, but she did not know that our baby had died. With eager anticipation, she asked me, "Where is your baby?"

I burst into tears and choked on the words: "My baby died."

You have no way of knowing when situations like this will occur. And you never know how you will react—sometimes you may be able to deal with them quite well. But they will happen—and it's all right to cry.

2. The funeral. Funeral services are primarily for the benefit of the survivor to help you accept the pain after having experienced the loss of your loved one. Carrying out the tasks associated with the funeral (including writing acknowledgment notes or cutting out newspaper clippings to compile a memory book) may help you work through your grief.

After Samuel died, I compiled a baby book with his pictures, his hair clippings, hand and footprints, birth and death certificate, obituaries, and other keepsakes. It helped me to accept his death and to share his memory with others who came to visit as I showed the book to them and talked about him.

3. Reviewing the past. As people come to visit, and during the funeral, many memories and stories about your loved one's life will be retold. You may want to write down some of these cherished memories for yourself and share them with other family members or friends. This may help others through the grieving process as well. Going through old photographs may be helpful as you review the past.

You should not be expected, nor expect yourself, to forget the past. By reviewing the memories you may reach the point where you can lay them to rest and be content to have had those experiences to cherish. However, don't live on memories. Should you find yourself becoming preoccupied with the past after a long period of time, you should consider professional counsel.

Because Samuel died at birth, we have few memories of him. So for me, part of reviewing the past included my thoughts and feelings during my pregnancy. When you lose someone you love it changes your life, no matter how short or long their stay on earth.

4. Dealing with anger. It is very common to feel anger when under the stress of bereavement. Anger seeks a target—someone or something to blame. You may feel angry at having been left behind. Perhaps you are angry at the doctors for not doing more to save your loved one. Or at a drunk driver. Perhaps you are angry at yourself for not being there to do something. You may even be angry at God.

Anger is a valid emotional response. Christians may find it especially difficult to accept the fact that they are angry. They may feel that anger is not an appropriate feeling for a Christian to experience, but that's as senseless as telling ourselves that we shouldn't feel hungry if we haven't eaten.

In his book, *Anger: Yours and Mine and What to Do About It*, Richard P. Walters says, "Anger is an emotion and a feeling—not a behavior. Feelings generally are neither right nor wrong in themselves, but they can lead to either right and constructive behavior or to wrong and destructive behavior."[3]

It is not wrong to feel angry. Even Jesus felt angry. As Christians we can learn to control our anger with the help of the indwelling Holy Spirit.

Your anger may take another form. Depression is anger turned inward. We may tell ourselves that being angry at someone else is not acceptable. Depression is a self-destructive form of anger in which you are the target rather than someone else or God.

If you are angry or depressed, the best place to begin is by acknowledging your feelings and by seeking a constructive way to deal with them. Be honest with yourself and with God. Acknowledge your feelings to God and ask for his help in dealing with them. Pray for the Lord's peace in your heart.

5. *Resolving guilt.* Feelings of guilt may surface at different times for various reasons. There are often things you wish you would have said or done. You may experience guilt if you think you could have somehow spared or saved your loved one from death. Although this may seem a logical conclusion depending upon the circumstances, it is helpful to remember that God is sovereign. Nothing happens of which he is not aware, and nothing happens outside of his control. What has happened—the death of your loved one—happened with his knowledge.

Sometimes death is explainable—often it is not. We cannot understand why a child dies or why a parent dies leaving young children behind. God alone understands, and he does see your grief. "But you, O God, do see trouble and grief; you consider it to take it in hand. The victim commits himself to you; you are the helper of the fatherless" (Psalm 10:14).

6. *Acceptance.* God desires for you to give your worries and cares to him, for these burdens were never meant to be carried alone. Sharing your burdens with God and with dear friends will help the healing process begin so that you can move toward acceptance.

It is a natural part of grieving to wonder, "Why did this happen to me; why did he have to die?" When I visited my doctor two weeks after Samuel died, he said that the one question I would have for a long time to come is "Why me?" We may never know the answer to such questions, but we do know that God allows both good and bad circumstances into our lives for our own benefit and for the benefit of others.

"Peace I leave with you; my peace I give you. I do not give to you as the world gives. Do not let your hearts be troubled and do not be afraid" (John 14:27). May you experience his peace.

Coping With the Loss

As a survivor, there are a number of strategies that may help you to cope with the loss of your loved one. Here are a few suggestions:

- Help others rather than dwelling on your own problems. We all need to feel useful and needed.

- Renew old friendships and develop new acquaintances, particularly with people of other generations.

- Join a support group in your church or community that offers companionship and opportunities for personal growth.

- Consider the future. Plan ahead and set some realistic goals for your life, but take one day at a time.

- Take care of yourself mentally, spiritually, and physically.

- Consider getting a pet for companionship. There are a number of programs available which match seniors to pets. Check with your local humane society.

•Accept and ask for help from others when needed.

•Maintain an active interest in family and friends.

Aloneness and Loneliness

As a survivor, you may be very lonely even amidst the busyness of life. Living alone can be very difficult especially if you are a widow or widower. You may feel as though no one else understands or has experienced what you are feeling. Yet, you are not alone. When you feel lonely, try to remember the Lord's promise, "I will never leave you nor forsake you" (Joshua 1:5). You have the Lord's word that he is always with you, especially in time of need. Allow the Holy Spirit, our Comforter, to minister to you.

Try to develop friendships with others who have experienced grief and understand the way you feel. If you do not know anyone who has lost a loved one, ask your pastor or funeral director if he can put you in touch with someone. Don't be afraid to pick up the telephone and call a friend when you are feeling alone and need to talk.

You should not be embarrassed to admit that you need the support of your family and friends during this difficult time in your life. As you go through the grieving process, the love and support you receive from your family and friends will be of tremendous help to you. However, your family and friends may not know when you are lonely. Therefore, it is important to let your family, friends, relatives, doctors, clergy, and others know how you feel and what support you need as you go through the grieving process.

Support Groups

There are many support groups which minister to the

needs of survivors. On pages 171-3 there are names and addresses of some of these groups. You may want to check your telephone directory to see which support groups are available in your area. Also, you may want to check with local churches to see what they offer. Perhaps you would even be interested in starting your own support group to minister to others in your community who have lost a loved one under similar circumstances or who are in your age group.

Do You Know *Him*?

Sorrowing and suffering are in vain if we do not experience the love and comfort God wants to give us. Perhaps you have not experienced God's comforting presence in your life because you do not really *know* him. Perhaps no one has told you *how* you can know God. If experiences you have gone through recently have caused you to want to know God, let me share with you the steps that will make that relationship a reality in your life:

In order to receive Jesus as your Savior, your Lord, and your Source of comfort, you must:

1. *Admit your need for a Savior.* Admit that you are a sinner and that you cannot save yourself. The Bible says, "For all have sinned, and come short of the glory of God" (Romans 3:23). The natural result of sin is death, "For the wages of sin is death (separation from God), but the gift of God is eternal life in Christ Jesus our Lord" (Romans 6:23).

2. *Be willing to turn from your sins (repent).* "If we confess our sins, he is faithful and just and will forgive us our sins and purify us from all unrighteousness" (1 John 1:9).

3. *Believe that Jesus Christ died for you on the Cross and rose from the grave.* "But God showed his love toward us, in that while we were yet sinners, Christ died for us" (Romans 5:8). He rose from the grave. "He is not here; he is risen, just as he said" (Matthew 28:6).

4. *Through prayer, invite Jesus Christ to come in and control your life (receive him as Lord and Savior).* "Yet to all who received him, to those who believed in his name, he gave the right to become children of God" (John 1:12).

The following is a prayer you can pray:

Dear Lord Jesus,

I know that I am a sinner and need your forgiveness. I believe that you died for my sins. I want to turn from my sins. I now invite you to come into my heart and life. I want to trust you as my Savior and follow you as my Lord.

If you prayed this prayer (or a similar prayer), you can be assured that you now have the gift of eternal life. It's not the words you pray but the attitude of your heart that matters to God. Your heart attitude must be genuine and sincere ". . . since he (God) knows the secrets of the heart" (Psalm 44:21).

"He who has the Son has life; he who does not have the Son of God does not have life. I write these things to you who believe in the name of the Son of God so that you may know that you have eternal life" (1 John 5:12-13). "If you believe that Jesus is the Christ—that he is God's Son and your Savior—then you are a child of God" (1 John 5:1, TLB).

If you want further help in the decision you have made, write to:

The Billy Graham Evangelistic Association
P.O. Box 779
Minneapolis, MN 55440-0779

or call: (612) 338-0500. Someone on our Christian Guidance staff would be happy to talk or pray with you!

Memory Ideas

After the death of a loved one, it is often important to the survivors to keep the loved one's memory alive. There are a number of ways you can do this:

1. Place photos of your loved one in a photo album for your family and friends to review and share their memories with you when they come to visit.
2. Preserve a flower or banner from the funeral service.
3. Donate money, time, or your talents to a charitable organization in your loved one's name (for which you may receive an acknowledgment that the gift was given in their name, and a certificate on which their name is inscribed).
4. Keep a journal of events and feelings regarding your loved one. This is also a good place to express your feelings of anger as you go through the grieving process. You could use your journal to record stories retold by friends and relatives about your loved one.
5. Donate money to your church to purchase a memorial window, furnishings, or library books. You may be able to place a plaque with the item stating that it was "given in loving memory of" the deceased.
6. Purchase a headstone or other marker to place at the gravesite. If there is no gravesite, memorial plaques can be placed in some hospitals and cemeteries.
7. Plant a memorial tree or flower bed. You may want to create your own memorial garden, either in your yard or with indoor plants.

What About the Holidays?

One of the most difficult times you may face as a survivor are the holidays whether it is the first or fifteenth one you've faced since losing your loved one. Holidays may be a difficult time for a number of reasons. Without your loved one, your attention may be drawn to past holidays. Reflecting on the past can sometimes be a painful reminder that now things will be different.

Traditions may change, entertaining may change, and your celebrations will be affected. Whenever change occurs in our lives, it takes time to adjust. You may find it helpful to plan ahead for the holidays. Take time to think about what you want to do and what you don't want to do during the holiday seasons. When the holidays arrive, say no to certain events if necessary. Do what makes you comfortable, not what others think you should do. Decide what you can handle, and gently let your needs be made known to your family and friends.

You may also decide that it is time to begin new traditions. Now may be the time to establish a new tradition in memory of the person you love. Buy a houseplant, plant a tree or flower, or give a gift in their memory. Perhaps there are special events you had always wanted to attend but had not done so. Perhaps you have friends you haven't seen for a long time. Now may be the time to renew old friendships and develop new acquaintances.

If you don't feel like celebrating the holidays, that's okay. If you're not ready this year, don't feel rushed or allow yourself to be pushed into things you'd rather not do. If you have children, though, you will want to consider their feelings and discuss this with them. A traditional family celebration may help you and your children to cope with the loss of the loved one. Because a number of changes take place as a result of death, it may be helpful to your children if the holidays remain as "normal" as possible.

If you are alone for the holidays, do something special for

yourself. Treat yourself to a play at the theater, a good book, a dinner at a nice restaurant, a long walk. Being alone doesn't mean that you will necessarily be lonely. It may be a good time to reflect upon life and to focus on the reasons to celebrate the season. You may have some wonderful quiet times with the Lord. If you know others who are alone, you may want to give them a call.

If you know that you do not want to be alone during the holidays, make plans not to be. You may want to travel to your family or friends' homes, spend time with your neighbors or church group, or invite guests to come and stay with you during the holidays. There are many activities that take place during the holidays; try to become involved in something. However, you will want to take care not to commit yourself to too many activities. You may end up exhausted and unfulfilled. By planning ahead, you may find yourself actually enjoying the holidays rather than just coping with them.

Time on Your Hands

As a survivor you may wonder what to do after the death of your loved one. You may have a lot of "time on your hands." If you are a widow or widower, you may have participated in many activities with your spouse. You may find that you no longer feel comfortable, especially if the activities were couple-oriented. Therefore, you may want to consider new activities you can pursue. Or perhaps you are already involved in activities to which you can now devote more of your time.

In most communities, there are many opportunities for involvement. These activities may include taking classes through community education, vocational school, college or university; finding a part-time or full-time job; becoming involved in a social club, community activities and events; ministering in your church or pursuing missions; volunteering your services at a hospital, senior citizen's center, non-profit organization, group home, or library; getting involved in your political party; or spending more time in leisure activities such as reading, hobbies, or crafts; exercising such as walking, swimming, tennis, golf, bowling, fishing, and other forms of recreation; or traveling within your state or province, country, or abroad.

As you consider how to fill your "free time," choose activities that are meaningful to you. Select something you firmly believe in—something to which you can commit yourself. But don't overdo it. As a survivor, you are going through one of the most stressful times in your life. Be good to yourself by selecting quality activities rather than quantity. Plan time for yourself when you can just be alone to think, reflect, and meditate. It is important to have quiet time every day—just you and God together.

Losing someone you love, taking care of the funeral arrangements, filing claims for survivors' benefits, making decisions regarding housing and investments, and the numerous other tasks involved are extremely stressful. It is quite understandable if you feel somewhat overwhelmed. Or you may even feel numb from all the emotion. This is natural. It is a part of the grieving process. (For more information about the grieving process, see the bibliography, page 185-6.)

Adjusting

As a survivor you have many new and exciting experiences ahead of you—although you may not feel this way right now. One of the most important things you can do while going through a stressful period in your life is to take care of yourself—physically, emotionally, and spiritually. Taking care of yourself includes your appearance, grooming, clothes, exercise, eating habits, etc. This may be especially difficult when it may become an ordeal just to get up in the morning.

If you are a widow or widower with children at home, you will have more responsibilities than ever before as you adjust to being a single parent. You will most likely need to find someone to assist you in caring for your children while you are at work, especially if they are young. If you are a widow or widower without children at home, you may have other areas of concern such as: coming home to an empty house; cooking, eating meals, and entertaining alone; home and auto repairs, especially if you haven't done them before; house-cleaning; and giving away some of your spouse's belongings.

Leaving a Legacy

It is natural after the loss of a loved one for survivors to think about their own death, and as they do life becomes even more precious. Often, priorities are rearranged, and commitments to family and friends become stronger. All too often we forget to tell our family and friends just how much they mean to us. You can leave a legacy of love for your survivors by spending as much time as possible with your family, friends, and loved ones *now*. "Teach us to number our days aright, that we may gain a heart of wisdom" (Psalm 90:12).

Preparing a legacy may include writing a special letter or recording a taped message to each person who is dear to you, and including it with your important papers. Have pictures taken of you and your loved ones together doing various activities that you enjoy, like baking cookies, raking leaves, reading a book, riding bikes, sight-seeing, or going on vacation.

We often remember people by the things they do. How wonderful to leave a legacy of memories of time spent with those you love, and of things you did to show them how much you care.

Whether you are the person planning an estate or a survivor settling an estate, we hope this book has served as a useful guide.

If perhaps you are one of the many people who do not want to even discuss planning your estate, not to mention making pre-need funeral arrangements, it is our prayer that this book has shown how valuable a gift those plans can be to your survivors.

The grieving process is never "easy." But many funeral directors agree that survivors who have the benefit of pre-need funeral arrangements and estate plans seem to work through their time of grieving more smoothly.

May God's grace be with you as you face difficult times in life. May he give you hope and encouragement to plan for tomorrow, and comfort and strength in sorrow as you live for today.

Appendix A

Following is a list of the information you will want to include in your records book:

Family Records

(For you and your spouse. Refer to forms on pages 144-8.)

1. Name, address, telephone number
2. Birth date
3. Marital status
4. Prior marriages/divorces
5. Citizenship
6. Social Security or Social Insurance number
7. Veterans Administration claim number
8. Employment, address, telephone number
9. Employment date, retirement date
10. Immediate supervisor
11. Armed forces branches and serial number
12. Discharge date
13. Educational information (degrees earned, honors and rewards received)
14. Children's names, birthdates
15. Other family members (names, addresses, phone numbers, and relationship)

Finances

1. Personal financial goals: What are your present/future needs, wants and dreams?
2. Personal action plan: How do you intend to accomplish your goals?
3. Financial planning priorities: What are your priorities? List them in order.
4. Prioritized financial objectives: Which goals are feasible based on your priorities and financial obligations?
5. Current annual income record
6. Current annual expenses record
7. Net worth statement—assets minus liabilities

Assets

1. Bonds, stocks, securities, mutual funds
2. Annuities and life income contracts
3. Individual Retirement Account (IRA)
4. Employer benefits
5. Organization or labor union benefits
6. Retirement benefits (pensions, Social Security, and veterans' benefits)
7. Real estate (house, vacation property, rental property, etc.)
8. Bank accounts (checking and savings)
9. U.S. savings bonds
10. Life insurance (cash value)
11. Savings and loans accounts
12. Credit union account
13. Vehicles (car, truck, boat, trailer, etc)
14. Clothing and personal belongings

Inventory of Valuables

(List model and year, identification number, approximate value, owner/location, desired recipient.)

1. Furniture
2. Jewelry
3. Antiques
4. Art
5. Collections (coins, stamps, etc.)
6. Furs
7. Other

Liabilities

1. Debts
2. Mortgages
3. Credit cards
4. Insurance premiums
5. Taxes
6. Other current bills
7. Charge accounts
8. Other loans (bank, credit union, or personal)

Estate Planning

1. Estate planning priorities: What are you retirement goals and objectives?
2. Estate planning basics—a will: Prepare a rough draft of your will to take to your attorney to be drafted.
3. Trust funds: List your trust funds, trustee, beneficiaries, etc.
4. Estate planning action plan: What are your present/future needs, wants, and dreams in the area of estate planning?

Insurance

1. Homeowner's or renter's real estate insurance
2. Life insurance
3. Health and disability insurance
4. Automobile/vehicle insurance
5. Pre-need funeral insurance (e.g., Purple Cross)

Medical Records

1. Medical insurance company (name, address, and telephone number)
2. Medical insurance policy number
3. Group policy number
4. Subscriber identification number
5. Other medical insurance
6. Disabilities
7. Major illnesses/operations
8. Blood type
9. Medical doctor (name, address, telephone number)
10. Dentist (name, address, telephone number)

11. Medical clinic and hospital (name, address, telephone number)
12. Organ/body donor preferences
13. Artificial life support preferences

Inventory of Possessions

(List manufacturer, model and year, identification or serial number, approximate value, owner/location, desired recipient.)

1. Automobiles/vehicles
2. Boats
3. Cameras
4. VCR
5. CB radio
6. Dishwasher
7. Washer/dryer
8. Jewelry
9. Microwave
10. Refrigerator/freezer
11. Fishing equipment
12. Hunting equipment
13. Guns/rifles
14. Recreational vehicle/motor home
15. Lawn mowers
16. Snowmobiles
17. Stereo
18. Sewing machine
19. Computer
20. Typewriter
21. Watches/clocks
22. Vacuum cleaner
23. Other

Important Documents

(Identification numbers and other pertinent information. Refer to form on page 142.)

1. Certified death certificates of deceased
2. Wills and codicils
3. Birth certificate of deceased, yourself, and children
4. Social Security card of deceased, yourself, and children (Social Insurance number, if in Canada)
5. Marriage certificate
6. Separation or divorce papers
7. Citizenship papers, if applicable
8. Passport or visa
9. Military discharge papers
10. Driver's license
11. Insurance policies
12. Bank records
13. Property deeds, abstracts
14. Vehicle titles
15. Income tax returns
16. Medical records
17. Disability claims
18. Adoption papers, if applicable
19. Legal papers
20. Funeral planning papers
21. Stock or bond certificates
22. Business agreements
23. Trust agreements
24. Annuity certificates
25. Mortgages and debts—how and when paid?
26. Employee handbook
27. Education records
28. List of employers and dates of employment
29. Religious affiliation, name of church and clergy
30. Memberships in organizations
31. Personal liabilities—what owed to whom
32. Credit cards and charge account names and numbers
33. Location of personal items such as jewelry or family heirlooms
34. Other

Location of Important Documents

Location of:

Birth certificate: _____

Children's birth certificates: _____

Marriage certificate: _____

Divorce papers: _____

Deeds and titles: _____

Mortgages and notes: _____

Wills/codicils: _____

Military discharge: _____

Income tax returns: _____

Annuities: _____

Trust agreements: _____

Savings bonds: _____

Guarantees/warranties: _____

Insurance policies: _____

Cemetery deeds: _____

Passport: _____

Safe-deposit/lock box: _____

Contracts: _____

Power of attorney: _____

Other documents: _____

Professional Advisors

(List names, addresses, and telephone numbers of business, legal, personal, and religious advisors.   Refer to form on page 147.)

1. Attorney
2. Clergy
3. Life insurance agent
4. Accountant
5. Financial planner
6. Stockbroker
7. Bank manager
8. Real estate advisor
9. Executor/executrix
10. Trust officer
11. Health insurance agent
12. Other

Funeral and Burial Arrangements

(List your wishes concerning your funeral and burial arrangements. Refer to forms on page 155-6.)

1. Funeral planning papers: List your wishes and outline your funeral in as much detail as possible. Include a copy of your Statement of Funeral Goods and Services Selected(page 157) indicating the arrangements you have made with your funeral director.
2. Important message to family: Write or tape record a message to your family.
3. Important message to friends: Write or tape record a message to your friends.
4. Your obituary: Write out your own obituary as a guideline for your survivors.

Personal Information Form

Name: _____ Date and place of birth: _____

Residence address: _____

_____

Resided in county: _____ Since: _____

Citizenship: _____ SSN: _____ Marital status: _____

Past residences: _____

_____

Place of employment: _____

Date of retirement: _____ Armed services serial no.: _____

Name of war or dates served: _____

Enlisted at: _____ Date: _____

Discharged at: _____ Date: _____

Location of discharge certificate: _____

Date and place of marriage: _____

Father's name: _____ Mother's name: _____

Address: _____ Address: _____

Father's birthplace: _____ Mother's birthplace: _____

Date of death: _____ Date of death: _____

Spouse's name: _____ Date and place of birth: _____

Maiden name: _____

Residence address: _____

Resided in county: _____ Since: _____

Citizenship: _____ SSN: _____ Marital status: _____

Place of employment: _____

Date of retirement: _____ Armed services serial no.: _____

Name of war or dates served: _____

Name of war or dates served: _____

Enlisted at: _____ Date: _____

Discharged at: _____ Date: _____

Location of discharge certificate: _____

Father's name: _____ Mother's name: _____

Address: _____

Address: _____

Father's birthplace: _____ Mother's birthplace: _____

Date of death: _____ Date of death: _____

Children's names, addresses, and dates of birth: _____

_____

_____

_____

_____

_____

Grandchildren/great-grandchildren's names, addresses, and dates of birth:

_____

_____

_____

_____

_____

_____

_____

_____

_____

_____

Employment Record
(List all past employers, dates of employment and your job titles.)

	Employer	Dates of Employment	Job Title
1.			
2.			
3.			
4.			
5.			
6.			
7.			
8.			
9.			
10.			

Financial Information Form

Your name: _____ Date: _____

Name of bank: _____ Account no.: _____

Address: _____

Banker's name: _____ Phone no.: _____

Safe-deposit box or lockbox: _____

                                      Location   Keys

Attorney's name: _____ Phone no.: _____

Address: _____

Insurance agent's name: _____ Phone no.: _____

Address: _____

Trust officer's name: _____ Phone no.: _____

Address: _____

Financial planner's name: _____ Phone no.: _____

Address: _____

Accountant's name _____ Phone no.: _____

Address _____

Executor's name: _____ Phone no.: _____

Address: _____

Alternate executor's name: _____ Phone no.: _____

Address: _____

Guardian's for minor children: _____

Address: _____

Estate distribution:

To spouse: _____

Address: _____

Percent or amount: _____

To children: _____

Address: _____

Percent or amount: _____

To other individuals: _____

Address: _____

Percent or amount: _____

To religious/charitable organizations: _____

Address: _____

Percent or amount: _____

Other information:

Appendix B

Request for Statement of Earnings

Form Approved
OMB No. 0960-0466

[ ] SP

Request for Earnings and Benefit Estimate Statement

[ ] Please check this box if you want to get your statement in Spanish instead of English.

Please print or type your answers. When you have completed the form, fold it and mail it to us.

1. Name shown on your Social Security card:

First Name _____ Middle Initial _____

Last Name Only

2. Your Social Security number as shown on your card:

[ ][ ][ ] [ ][ ] [ ][ ][ ][ ]

3. Your date of birth

[ ][ ] [ ][ ] [ ][ ]
Month   Day   Year

4. Other Social Security numbers you have used:

[ ][ ][ ] [ ][ ] [ ][ ][ ][ ]
[ ][ ][ ] [ ][ ] [ ][ ][ ][ ]

5. Your sex: [ ] Male [ ] Female

6. Other names you have used *(including a maiden name):*

_____

For items 7 and 9 show only earnings covered by Social Security. Do NOT include wages from State, local or Federal Government employment that are NOT covered for Social Security or that are covered ONLY by Medicare.

7. Show your actual earnings (wages and/or net self-employment income) for last year and your estimated earnings for this year.

A. Last year's actual earnings: *(Dollars Only)*

$ [ ][ ][ ] , [ ][ ][ ] . 0 0

B. This year's estimated earnings: *(Dollars Only)*

$ [ ][ ][ ] , [ ][ ][ ] . 0 0

8. Show the age at which you plan to stop working.

[ ][ ]
(Show only one age)

9. Below, show the average yearly amount (not you total future lifetime earnings) that you think you will earn between now and when you plan to stop working. Include cost-of-living, performance or scheduled pay increases or bonuses.

If you expect to earn significantly more or less in the future due to promotions, job changes, part-time work, or an absence from the work force, enter the amount that most closely reflects your future average yearly earnings.

If you don't expect any significant changes, show the same amount you are earning now (the amount in 7B).

Future average yearly earnings: *(Dollars Only)*

$ [ ][ ][ ] , [ ][ ][ ] . 0 0

10. Address where you want us to send the statement.

Name _____

Street Address (Include Apt. No., P.O. Box, or Rural Route) _____

City _____ State _____ Zip Code _____

Notice:
I am asking for information about my own Social Security record or the record of a person I am authorized to represent. I understand that when requesting information on a deceased person, I must include proof of death and relationship or appointment. I further understand that if I deliberately request information under false pretenses , I may be guilty of a Federal crime and could be fined and/or imprisoned. I authorize you to use a contractor to send the statement of earnings and benefit estimates to the person named in item 10.

▲

Please sign your name (Do Not Print)

_____

Date _____ (Area Code) Daytime Telephone No. _____

Form **SSA-7004-SM** (4-95) Destroy prior editions   ♻ Printed on recycled paper

Appendix C

Investment objective

Before you invest, you will want to take time to consider what your objective is in investing. You will want to ask yourself the following questions:

_____ Do you want to make all the investment decisions yourself? Are you able to handle the responsibility of managing your own investments?

_____ Or would you prefer to have the expertise of a professional? It will be helpful to indicate your investment goals to your advisor. Indicate below the principal objective you want your professional investment manager to follow.

I want my investment manager to invest with the following principal objective:

_____ I. Current Yield
Investments would include fixed income U.S. government or U.S. government agency securities, corporate bonds, and federally insured deposits.

_____ II. Growth
Investments would include good quality corporate common stock or mutual funds that produce little or no current ordinary income but have a history of significant appreciation in value.

_____ III. Tax Exempt Income
Investments would include good quality state or local government bonds.

Appendix D

Duties of an Executor

Collects Assets and Gathers Information:
1. Studies the Will
   a. notifies the witnesses
   b. meets with family members, attorney and others to discuss provisions of the will
2. Arranges for Probate of Will (if applicable)
   a. arranges for notice to creditors
   b. asks Post Office to forward mail
   c. notifies banks, investment brokers and others
   d. arranges for bond, if necessary
   e. opens bank accounts for estate
   f. discontinues telephone and other utilities when advisable
3. Assembles Inventories and Takes Custody of Assets
   a. searches for assets
   b. lists safe-deposit box contents
   c. inspects real estate, studies leases, mortgages and other contracts
   d. has assets appraised for value
   e. files veteran's claims, Social Security benefits and life insurance payable to the estate
   f. examines policies of insurance on real estate and personal property, has policies endorsed to the estate and coverage modified as necessary
   g. obtains all cancelled checks
   h. studies decedent's income tax returns for previous three years
4. Determines Debts and Claims Against the Estate
   a. collects all money, income due decedent or estate
   b. examines each claim against the estate for validity
   c. defends against any lawsuits
   d. makes payment of approved debts and claims against the estate

Administers (Manages) the Estate:
1. Financial Matters
   a. estimates cash needed to settle estate, selects assets to be sold to raise cash
   b. collects rent and maintains real estate
2. Bookkeeping
   a. sets up bookkeeping records
   b. examines business books/records
   c. supervises family-owned business
3. Legal Business
   a. meets with attorneys
   b. through attorney, files necessary documents with the court and arranges appropriate notices
   c. requests allowance from court for support of decedent's family

Determines and Pays all Taxes:
1. Income Taxes
   a. files return for decedent
   b. files estate income tax return during administration period
   c. prepares for the audit by tax authorities of income tax returns filed by decedent
   d. decides whether to take certain medical expenses as an income or estate tax deduction
2. Death Taxes (not applicable in Canada)
   a. considers whether living trusts or gifts made by decedent are taxable in the estate
   b. files the federal preliminary estate tax notice
   c. files state inheritance or estate tax returns as may be required
   d. decides whether administration expenses are to be deducted from federal income or estate tax
   e. files federal estate tax return and any other documents that may be required
   f. determines claims against persons who receive property outside of the will for their share of death taxes

Distributes the Estate:
1. determines who is entitled to share in the estate
2. sells assets to raise cash
3. determines distribution of assets
4. pays all final costs
5. arranges securities transfers
6. prepares detailed final account for the court
7. obtains and files receipts from all beneficiaries

What Your Executor Needs to Know About You

You can be of great assistance to your executor by providing them with the following information:

1. Your legal name and permanent address.
2. Addresses of your other residences, time you spend in each, where you're registered to vote.
3. Date and place of your birth.
4. The Social Security or Social Insurance numbers of you and your spouse.
5. Your spouse's legal name.
6. The date and place of your marriage and place where your marriage license can be found.
7. If married previously, give name of former or deceased spouse. If divorced, give place of divorce, whether contested, and who brought the action. If separated by agreement or court action, give all details including where your separation agreement can be found.
8. A copy of a prenuptial agreement if you entered into one.
9. List names, addresses, and ages of your immediate relatives and indicate whether any are incompetent.
10. List names and addresses of beneficiaries.
11. If you have a trust or are a beneficiary under a trust, have a copy of the trust available.
12. Your accountant's and attorney's names and addresses.
13. Your employer's name and address.
14. State whether you are entitled to a pension or any other employment benefits. Are any of these benefits payable on your death? Provide a copy of any related documents.
15. List life insurance policies.
16. List real estate and any other assets you own.
17. Give approximate amount of your debts, include names and addresses of those you owe.

Appendix E

Funeral Checklist

I. Notification

☐ A. Doctor and/or undertaker
☐ B. Family, friends, and relatives
☐ C. Pastor or clergy
☐ D. Deceased's employer and trade union
☐ E. Executor (personal representative)
☐ F. Deceased's lawyer, banker, accountant, stockbroker, insurance agents, charitable organizations, and other business contacts
☐ G. Civic groups of which deceased was a member
☐ H. Newspapers

II. Preparation

☐ A. Locate deceased's funeral planning papers regarding funeral wishes
☐ B. Obtain eight to ten certified copies of the death certificate

III. Body Disposition

☐ A. Call funeral or memorial society director or medical research institution for removal of body
☐ B. Decide on kind of disposition (burial, entombment, cremation, or donation of body to medical institute)

IV. Funeral or Memorial Service

☐ A. Outline service in as much detail as possible, select clothing
☐ B. Decide on place, who to officiate, pallbearers, kind of service, flowers, transportation, music, musicians and organist, Scripture, prayer, etc., and notify the appropriate persons
☐ C. Decide what should be included in the obituary regarding the service and send the information to the newspapers (funeral director may do this for you for a fee)
☐ D. Make appointment with funeral or memorial society director
☐ E. Arrange for after-service luncheon or gathering of friends and relatives

V. Prices

☐ A. Consider how much the funeral arrangements or memorial service will cost
☐ B. Determine how much you can afford to spend and work within that financial framework
☐ C. Compare prices and determine which services, if any, you or your survivors can handle

VI. Visit Funeral Home

☐ A. Make arrangements with funeral director
☐ B. Take a friend, relative, or other advisor with you
☐ C. Select casket or urn, if necessary
☐ D. Set date and time for viewal service, if desired

VII. Cemetery or Crematorium

☐ A. Compare prices at several cemeteries or crematoriums
☐ B. Make an appointment with cemetery or crematorium
☐ C. Purchase cemetery lot, crypt, and vault (if necessary)
☐ D. Determine cemetery or crematorium requirements and charges
☐ E. Make arrangements for burial, entombment, or cremation

VIII. Other Duties

☐ A. Make arrangements for out-of-town family members or guests
☐ B. Arrange for disposition of flowers after funeral ceremony
☐ C. Keep track of sympathy cards for later acknowledgment
☐ D. Take care of deceased's home and personal property until executor arrives to take over the responsibilities
☐ E. Meet with attorney to begin probate proceedings

IX. After Funeral or Memorial Service

☐ A. Send notes to acknowledge expressions of sympathy
☐ B. Determine what death benefits (Social Security, life insurance, veterans, pension, etc.) are available to you as a survivor and file claims with appropriate agencies
☐ C. Cancel and destroy credit cards in the name of the deceased

Funeral Planning Worksheet

Place of service: _____

Church denomination: _____

Clergy's name _____

Address: _____ Phone no.: _____

Military or fraternal organization: _____

Type of service _____ ☐ Open ☐ Closed

Casket: _____ Color (ext.): _____

Flag: ☐ Yes   ☐ No.

Folded, place at head: ☐ Yes   ☐ No   Draped over casket: ☐ Yes   ☐ No.

Organist/musicians: _____

Music selections: _____

Scripture selections: _____

Clothing: _____

Jewelry: _____ Return to: _____

Wedding ring: _____ Return to: _____

Eye glasses: _____ Return to: _____

Pallbearers and honorary pallbearers: _____

_____

Cemetery Decisions

Location of ownership certificate (deed for cemetery property):

_____

Name of cemetery: _____

Military or fraternal organization: _____

Prefer: ☐ Mausoleum entombment ☐ Lawn crypts ☐ Spaces

Actual description of cemetery property: _____

_____

Crypt or space: _____ Tier or lot: _____

Mausoleum or lawn: _____ Vault: _____

Flower container: _____ Flag: _____

Memorial marker: _____

Inscription: _____

_____

Emblem: _____ Flowers: _____

Special instructions: _____

Signed: _____ Date: _____

Appendix F

Statement of Funeral Goods and Services Selected

A) Forwarding of remains to another funeral home . $ _____

   Receiving of remains from another funeral home $ _____

   Direct cremation .... $ _____

   Immediate burial .... $ _____

   Services of funeral director, staff .... $ _____

   Embalming .... $ _____

   Other care and preparation .... $ _____

   Special care of autopsied remains .... $ _____

   Sanitation only (no embalming) .... $ _____

   Beautician (hairdresser) .... $ _____

   Transfer to church .... $ _____

   Basic use of facilities and specialized equipment $ _____

        For funeral ceremony .... $ _____

        For visitation or viewing................................. $ _____

        Preparation room (shelter of remains) .... $ _____

   Transfer of remains to funeral chapel .... $ _____

   Funeral chapel .... $ _____

   Funeral coach .... $ _____

   Service car .... $ _____

   Pallbearers car .... $ _____

   Floral delivery car .... $ _____

   Cemetery delivery .... $ _____

   Church delivery .... $ _____

   Additional limousines .... $ _____

   Miscellaneous merchandise:

        Acknowledgment cards .... $ _____

        Visitor register .... $ _____

        Prayer cards .... $ _____

        Memorial folders .... $ _____

        Cross or crucifix .... $ _____

        Clothing .... $ _____

        Candles .... $ _____

B) Casket (as selected) .... $ _____
C) Outer burial container
    (as selected) .... $ _____
                     SUBTOTAL (A,B, C) $ _____
D) Other
    _____ $ _____
    _____ $ _____
                     SUBTOTAL (D) .... $ _____ $ _____
E) Cash advance items:
    Cemetery .... $ _____
    Church or clergy .... $ _____
    Music .... $ _____
    Obituary notices (estimate) .... $ _____
    Motorcycle escort .... $ _____
    Certified copies of death certificate .... $ _____
    Casket engraving .... $ _____
    Flowers .... $ _____
    _____ $ _____
    _____ $ _____
    _____ $ _____
                    SUBTOTAL (E) $ _____
       TOTAL AMOUNT (A,B, C, D& E) $ _____

Appendix G

Sample Certificate of Death

MINNESOTA DEPARTMENT OF HEALTH
Section of Vital Statistics
CERTIFICATE OF DEATH

LOCAL FILE NUMBER   STATE FILE NUMBER

1. DECEDENT'S NAME (first, middle, last)		2. SEX	3. DATE OF DEATH (month, day, year)	4. TIME OF DEATH

5. SOCIAL SECURITY NUMBER	6a. AGE – Last Birthday (years)	6b. UNDER 1 YEAR (months / days)	6c. UNDER 1 DAY (hours / minutes)	7. DATE OF BIRTH (month, day, year)

8. BIRTHPLACE (city and state or foreign country) | **9. WAS DECEDENT EVER IN U.S. ARMED FORCES?** (specify yes or no) | **10a. PLACE OF DEATH** (check only one see instructions on other side) — HOSPITAL ☐ ER/Outpatient ☐ Inpatient ☐ DOA OTHER ☐ Nursing home ☐ Residence ☐ Other (specify)

10b. FACILITY NAME (if not institution, give street and number) | **10c. CITY OR TOWNSHIP OF DEATH** | **10d. COUNTY OF DEATH**

11. MARITAL STATUS — Married, Never Married, Widowed, Divorced (specify) | **12. SPOUSE** — Name (if wife, give maiden name) | **13a. DECEDENT'S USUAL OCCUPATION** (give kind of work done during most of working life. Do not use retired)

13b. KIND OF BUSINESS/INDUSTRY | **14a. RESIDENCE — State** | **14b. COUNTY**

14c. CITY OR TOWNSHIP

14d. STREET AND NUMBER | **14e. INSIDE CITY LIMITS?** (specify yes or no) | **14f. ZIP CODE** | **15. WAS DECEDENT OF HISPANIC ORIGIN?** (specify yes or no — if yes, specify Cuban, Mexican, Puerto Rican, etc.) ☐ Yes ☐ No

16. RACE (see instructions on other side) | **17. DECEDENT'S EDUCATION** (specify only highest grade completed) Elementary/Secondary (0-12) College (1-4 or 5+) | **18. FATHER'S NAME** (first, middle, last)

19. MOTHER'S NAME (first, middle, maiden surname) | **20a. INFORMANT'S NAME** (type/print) | **20b. INFORMANT'S MAILING ADDRESS** Street and Number or Rural Route Number, City, State, Zip Code

21a. METHOD OF DISPOSITION ☐ Burial ☐ Cremation ☐ Removal from state ☐ Donation ☐ Other (specify)

21b. PLACE OF DISPOSITION (name of cemetery, crematory, or other place) | **21c. LOCATION** - City or Township, State | **22a. SIGNATURE OF FUNERAL DIRECTOR OR MORTICIAN**

22b. LICENSE NUMBER (of Funeral Service) | **23. NAME AND ADDRESS OF FUNERAL SERVICE** | **24a. CERTIFIER** (check only one) ☐ CERTIFYING PHYSICIAN To the best of my knowledge, death occurred at the place and time and on the date stated above and due to the causes and in the manner stated.

24b. SIGNATURE Physician, Medical Examiner or Coroner | **24c. LICENSE NUMBER** (of physician) | **24d. DATE SIGNED** (month, day, year) | ☐ MEDICAL EXAMINER/CORONER on the basis of examination and/or investigation, in my opinion, death occurred at the time, date, and place and due to the cause(s) and manner as stated.

25. NAME AND ADDRESS OF PHYSICIAN, MEDICAL EXAMINER OR CORONER | **26. REGISTRAR'S SIGNATURE**

27. DATE FILED (month, day, year)

28. CAUSE OF DEATH
PART I Enter the diseases, injuries or complications that caused the death. Do not enter the mode of dying, such as cardiac or respiratory arrest, shock, or heart failure. List only one cause on each line. | If diagnosis deferred ☐ Check box | Approximate interval between onset and death

IMMEDIATE CAUSE (final disease or condition resulting in death) a. _____ due to or as a consequence of:

Sequentially list conditions, if any, leading to immediate cause Enter UNDERLYING CAUSE (disease or injury that initiated events resulting in death) LAST b. _____ due to or as a consequence of:

c. _____

PART II. OTHER SIGNIFICANT CONDITIONS contributing to death but not resulting in the underlying cause given in PART I. | **29a. WAS CASE REFERRED TO MEDICAL EXAMINER/CORONER?** ☐ Yes ☐ No | **29b. WAS AN AUTOPSY PERFORMED?** ☐ Yes ☐ No | **29c. WERE AUTOPSY FINDINGS AVAILABLE PRIOR TO COMPLETION OF CAUSE OF DEATH?** ☐ Yes ☐ No

30. MANNER OF DEATH ☐ Natural ☐ Accident ☐ Suicide ☐ Homicide ☐ Pending investigation ☐ Could not be determined | **31a. DATE OF INJURY** (month, day, year) | **31b. TIME OF INJURY** ___ M

31c. INJURY AT WORK? ☐ Yes ☐ No | **31d. DESCRIBE HOW INJURY OCCURRED**

31e. PLACE OF INJURY - At home, farm, street, factory, office building, etc. (specify) | **31f. LOCATION** - (street and number) ___ city or township, state

HE-00110-03 REV. (1/89)

SAMPLE

Appendix H

Social Security Benefits

Some of the evidence you may need in order to apply for Social Security benefits:

1. Your Social Security number (Social Insurance number, in Canada) and the deceased's Social Security number
2. Proof of your age (birth certificate)
3. Birth certificate of the deceased
4. Proof of marriage (marriage license), if you are applying for widow's or widower's benefits
5. Proof of the deceased's death (certified death certificate)
6. Children's birth certificates, if they are applying for benefits
7. Deceased's Form W-2 (or federal tax return, if self-employed) for the most recent tax year
8. Proof of support if you are applying for benefits as a dependent parent or grandchild of the deceased
9. Checkbook or savings passbook for direct deposit of benefit checks
10. Proof of pre-1968 military service
11. Proof of relationship to deceased
12. Proof of disability
13. Proof of school attendance if you are currently a student

Veterans' Benefits

Some of the evidence you may need in order to apply for veterans' benefits:

1. Certified copy of death certificate
2. Veteran's discharge papers
3. Itemized funeral bill receipt
4. Marriage certificate
5. Birth certificates of minor children

Appendix I

Budget Income Worksheet

1. Salary/wages
2. Social Security
3. Welfare or other government income
4. Pension plan
5. Savings account
6. Other investments
7. Stocks, bonds, investment interest
8. IRA
9. Keogh plan
10. Life insurance (cash value)
11. Profit-sharing plan
12. Sale of business
13. Sale of possessions
14. Sale of real estate (home, property, etc.)
15. Annuities, trusts
16. Other

   Total Annual Income

Budget Expenses Worksheet

1. Rent or mortgage
2. Food
3. Clothing
4. Utilities (gas, water, electric, sewer, etc.)
5. Appliances
6. Furniture
7. Automobiles
8. Telephone
9. Medical
10. Entertainment
11. Personal items
12. Taxes
13. Gifts
14. Home maintenance and repairs
15. Insurance premiums (auto, home, health, life)
16. Other

   Total Annual Expenses

Appendix J

Housing Checklist

This checklist will help you to evaluate your current housing situation and new housing options you are considering. Would the following be readily available:

1. Medical facilities
2. Public transportation
3. Suitable climate
4. Recreation (golf, swimming, tennis, parks, etc.)
5. Clubs and social activities
6. Community involvement (volunteer opportunities)
7. Church (public worship and ministry opportunities)
8. Pets (are you able to have pets if you so desire?)
9. Neighbors with similar interests and lifestyles
10. Emergency protection (police, fire, ambulance)
11. Education (vocational, community college)
12. Employment opportunities (part-time or full-time)
13. Entertainment (theaters, movies, etc.)
14. Family and friends nearby
15. Shopping malls
16 Drinking water acceptable
17. Parking space and traffic
18. Heating/air conditioning costs
19. Utilities costs (garbage, water, electricity, etc.)
20. Pollution control (air, noise, landscape)

Resource List

Chapter 1

Financial Planning

International Association for Financial Planning
Two Concourse Parkway, Suite 800
Atlanta, GA 30328
(404) 256-8668

Certified Public Accountants

American Institute of Certified Public Accountants
1211 Avenue of the Americas
New York, NY 10036-8775
(212) 596-6200

Life Insurance in the United States

The National Underwriter Company
505 Guest Street
Cincinnati, OH 45203
(513) 721-2140

Life Insurance in Canada

Institute of Chartered Life Underwriters of Canada
41 Lesmill Road
Don Mills, ON M3B 2T3
(416) 444-5251

Long-term Care and Nursing Home Care Insurance

American Council of Life Insurance (ACLI)/
Health Insurance Association of America (HIAA)
1001 Pennsylvania Avenue, NW
Washington, DC 20004-2599
(202) 624-2000

Chapter 2

Better Business Bureaus in the United States & Canada

Council of Better Business Bureaus
4200 Wilson Boulevard, Suite 800
Arlington, VA 22203-1804
(703) 276-0100

National Headquarters for Canadian Bureaus
Suite 209
115 Apple Creek Boulevard
Markham, ON L3R 6C9
(905) 415-1750

Attorneys/Legal Matters

American Bar Association
750 North Lakeshore Drive
Chicago, IL 60611
(312) 988-5000

Canadian Bar Association
Suite 200, 20 Toronto Street
Toronto, ON M5C 2B8
(416) 869-1047

Chapter 3

Funeral and Memorial Societies

The Continental Association of Funeral
and Memorial Societies (CAFMS)
6900 Lost Lake Road
Egg Harbor, WI 54209
(414) 868-3136

CAFMS is a consumer organization that provides information about alternatives for funeral or non-funeral dispositions. It encourages advance planning and cost efficiency. The CAFMS sister organization in Canada is MSAC.

The Memorial Society Association of Canada (MSAC)
55 Saint Phillips Road
Etobicoke, ON M9P 2N8
(416) 241-6274

National Selected Morticians (NSM)
5 Riviera Drive, Suite 340
Northbrook, IL 60062-8009
(708) 559-9569

NSM is a national association of funeral firms in which membership is by invitation only and is conditioned upon the commitment of each firm to comply with the association's Code of Good Funeral Practice. Consumers may request a variety of publications through NSM's affiliate, the Consumer Information Bureau, Inc.

National Funeral Directors Association (NFDA)
11121 West Oklahoma Ave.
Milwaukee, WI 53227
(414) 541-2500

NFDA is the largest educational and professional association of funeral directors. Established in 1882, it has 14,000 members throughout the United States.

Cremation Association of North America (CANA)
401 North Michigan Avenue
Chicago, IL 60611
(312) 644-6610

CANA is an association of crematories, cemeteries, and funeral homes that offer cremation. More than six hundred members belong who own and operate crematories and who encourage the concept of memorialization.

International Order of the Golden Rule (IOGR)
1000 Churchill Road
P.O. Box 3586
Springfield, IL 62708
(217) 793-3322

IOGR, established in 1928, is an international association of independent funeral homes in which membership is by invitation or through application. However, IOGR does not solicit a new member without a member recommendation. More than 1200 funeral homes are members of IOGR.

Pre-Arrangement Interment Association of America (PIAA)
1130 Connecticut Avenue Northwest
Washington, DC 20037
(202) 223-2223

PIAA is a national association with more than 600 members in the cemetery and funeral home business. The primary purpose of the organization is to provide prearrangement purchases of funeral and cemetery goods and services.

Funeral Service Consumer Action Program (ThanaCAP)
11121 West Oklahoma Avenue
Milwaukee, WI 53227
(414) 541-2500

ThanaCAP is an independent organization sponsored by the National Funeral Directors Association (listed above) that channels and arbitrates consumer complaints involving funeral directors. It will handle complaints whether or not the funeral director is a member of NFDA.

Conference of Funeral Service Examining Boards (CFSEB)
2404 Washington Boulevard, Suite 1000
Ogden, UT 84401
(801) 392-7771

CFSEB is an association which represents the licensing boards of forty-seven states. CFSEB provides information on the laws of the various states and accepts and responds to consumer inquiries or complaints about funeral providers.

Cemeteries

Cemetery Consumer Service Council
P.O. Box 2028
Reston, VA 22090
(703) 391-8407

Monuments

> Monument Builders of North America
> 1740 Ridge Avenue
> Evanston, IL 60201
> (708) 803-8800

Organ Donor Information

If you are interested in becoming an organ donor, you should write:

> The Living Bank
> P.O. Box 6725
> Houston, TX 77265
> 1-800-528-2971 (toll free)
> In Texas, call (713) 528-2971

> Life Source
> 3433 Broadway St., NE
> Suite 260
> Minneapolis, MN 55413
> 1-800-247-4273

> Medic Alert Organ Donor Program
> 2323 Colorado Avenue
> Turlock, CA 95382
> (209) 668-3333

Medic Alert is a nonprofit organization dedicated to saving lives. Founded in 1956 by a physician, Medic Alert is one of the most comprehensive emergency medical identification systems in the world.

Chapter 4

Widows' Organizations

> Widowed Persons Service
> Sinai Hospital
> Greenspring & Belvedere Avenues
> Baltimore, MD 21215
> (410) 578-5678

Widowed Information & Consultation Services (WICS)
Family Services
15417 First Avenue South
Seattle, WA 98148
(206) 246-6142

Chapter 5

Survivors' Social Security Benefits

U.S. Department of Health and Human Services
Social Security Administration
Baltimore, MD 21235
1-800-772-1213

Veterans' and Dependents' Benefits

Veterans Administration (United States)
Washington, DC 20420
1-800-669-8477

Department of Veterans Affairs (Canada)
East Memorial Building
Lyon and Wellington Streets
Ottawa, ON K1A 0P4

Life Insurance Claim Disputes

For claims or disputes concerning life insurance, contact your state insurance commissioner (United States) or provincial superintendent of insurance (Canada):

Insurance Commissioner
State Department of Insurance
(Statehouse address)
(City, State, Zip Code)

Superintendent of Insurance
Province Department of Insurance
(Street address)
(City, Province, Postal Code)

Medicare and Medicaid

U.S. Department of Health and Human Services
Health Care Financing Administration (HCFA)
Social Security Administration
Baltimore, MD 21235
call between 8 A.M. and midnight
eastern standard time to ask specific questions
1-800-772-1213

HCFA is the federal agency that administers Medicare.

To obtain a free booklet, *Medicare: What It Will and Will Not Pay For*, send a self-addressed envelope to:

The American Society of Internal Medicine (ASIM)
Suite 500
1101 Vermont Avenue, NW
Washington, DC 20005

Chapter 6

Housing for Seniors

American Association of Homes and Services
for the Aging (AAHA)
901 E Street, NW, Suite 500
Washington, DC 20004-2837
(202) 783-2242

AAHA is the national organization of nonprofit homes and services for seniors. Its membership consists of 3,300 nursing homes, residential retirement complexes, continuing care (life-care) facilities, low-income rental housing, and community service organizations. In addition, it has eight hundred associate members. Thirty-eight affiliated state associations complete AAHA's membership.

Home Building

National Association of Home Builders
1201 15th Street, NW
Washington, DC 20005
(202) 822-0409 (DC)
1-800-368-5242 (toll free)

Shared Housing

National Shared Housing Resource Center (NSHRC)
321 East 25th Street
Baltimore, MD 21218
(410) 235-4454

NSHRC Inc. was founded in 1981 to assist in increasing the availability of shared housing programs throughout the United States. Toward this end, NSHRC offers a variety of shared housing services through local regional and national projects.

Home Equity Conversion

National Center for Home Equity Conversion
7373 147th Street W
Apple Valley, MN 55124
(612) 953-4474

Home Care

National Association of Home Care (NAHC)
228 Seventh Street, SE
Washington, DC 20003
(202) 547-7424

NAHC and its member agencies work to promote excellence in home care.

Cooperative Housing

National Association of Housing Cooperatives
2501 "M" Street, NW, Suite 451
Washington, DC 20037

Mobile/Manufactured Homes

Manufactured Housing Institute (MHI)
1745 Jefferson Davis Highway, Suite 511
Arlington, VA 22202
(703) 979-6620

MHI is a nonprofit national trade association of manufactured home builders and their suppliers. Some 160 supplier firms are members.

Nursing Homes and Long-Term Care Facilities

American Health Care Association (AHCA)
1201 "L" Street, NW
Washington, DC 20005
(202) 842-4444

AHCA is the nation's largest nonprofit federation of licensed nursing homes and allied long-term care facilities representing nine thousand facility members. AHCA was founded in 1949 and services approximately 900,000 senior citizens.

Chapter 7

Support Groups

There are many support groups available for those who have lost a loved one. Some of these are:

Theos Foundations, Inc.
(They Help Each Other Spiritually)
1301 Clark Building
715 Liberty Avenue
Pittsburgh, PA 15222
(412) 471-7779

American Association of Suicidology
4201 Connecticut Avenue, Suite 310
Washington, DC 20008
(202) 237-2280

Emotions Anonymous
P.O. Box 4245
St. Paul, MN 55104
(612) 647-9712

Recovery, Inc.
802 North Dearborn
Chicago, IL 60610
(312) 337-5661

RTS Bereavement Services
Gunderson Lutheran Medical Service
1910 South Street
La Crosse, WI 54601
(608) 785-0530, ext. 4747

The Compassionate Friends, Inc.
National Headquarters
900 Jorie Boulevard
Oak Brook, IL 60521-2213
(708) 990-0010

Hoping
Sparrow Hospital
1215 East Michigan Avenue
Lansing, MI 48912-1811
(517) 483-2700

Minnesota Sudden Infant Death Syndrome Foundation
Children's Health
2525 Chicago Avenue South
Minneapolis, MN 55404
(612) 813-6285

Share
St. John's Hospital
800 E. Carpenter Street
Springfield, IL 62702
(217) 544-6464, ext. 4500

Pregnancy and Infant Loss Center
1421 Wayzata Boulevard
Wayzata, MN 55391
(612) 473-9372

Additional Resources

Aging

National Council on the Aging (NCOA)
409 Third Street, SW
Washington, DC 20024-3200
(202) 479-1200

NCOA, founded in 1950, is a nonprofit organization that has been the national resource for information, training, technical assistance, advocacy, publications, and research on every aspect of aging. Write to NCOA for a catalog listing the many publications they have available on various issues related to aging.

Gray Panthers
2025 Pennsylvania Avenue
Suite 281
Washington, DC 20006
(202) 466-3132

The Gray Panthers was founded in 1970 by social activist Maggie Kuhn and five friends. Gray Panthers is a national grass-roots organization with young, old, and middle-aged members (over seventy thousand national members plus a local chapter of nearly ten thousand). Gray Panthers works to promote positive attitudes toward aging.

Consumer Information

National Consumers League (NCL)
Suite 516
815 15th Street, NW
Washington, DC 20005
(202) 639-8140

NCL, founded in 1899, is a nonprofit, membership organization representing consumers and workers on the federal level. The League works to win and maintain health and safety protections and to promote fairness at the marketplace and workplace.

Public Citizen (PC)
2000 "P" Street, NW, Suite 708
Washington, DC 20036
(202) 833-3000

PC, founded by Ralph Nader in 1971, is a nonprofit organization representing consumer rights in the marketplace, for safe products, for a healthy environment and workplace, for clean and safe energy sources, and for corporate and government accountability.

To obtain a catalog of more than two hundred federal consumer publications, write to:

Consumer Information Center
Public Documents Distribution Center
P.O. Box 100
Pueblo, CO 81002

When ordering only free booklets, direct your request to: S. James. (Remember to include the $1.00 fee when ordering two or more free booklets.) When ordering only sales booklets or both free and sales booklets, direct your request to: R. Woods.

To obtain a catalog listing forms and documents which have been printed by the U.S. government, contact:

Superintendent of Documents
U.S. Government Printing Office
P.O. Box 371954
Pittsburgh, PA 15250-7954
(202) 512-1803

For information regarding consumer protection, contact:

Federal Trade Commission
Office of Consumer and Business Education
Bureau of Consumer Protection
6 Pennsylvania Avenue, NW
Washington, DC 20580

National Senior Organizations

AARP (American Association of Retired Persons)
National Activities Office
601 "E" Street, NW
Washington, DC 20049

Widowed Persons Service
1711 North Parham Road
Richmond, VA 23229-4606
(804) 288-4474

National Council of Senior Citizens (NCSC)
1331 "F" Street
Washington, DC 20004
(202) 624-9500

Older Women's League (OWL)
666 11th Street, NW
Washington, DC 20005
(202) 783-6686

OWL, founded in 1980, is the first national grassroots membership organization to focus exclusively on women as they age.

National Association of State Units on Aging (NASUA)
16th and "K" Streets, NW
Washington, DC 20025
(202) 737-1913

NASUA, founded in 1964, is a national public interest organization dedicated to providing general and specialized information, technical assistance, and professional development support to State Units on Aging. The membership of the Association is comprised of fifty-seven state and territorial government units.

United Seniors Health Cooperative (USHC)
1331 "H" Street
Washington, DC 20005
(202) 393-6222

Endnotes

Chapter 1: Financial Planning

1. *The Consumer's Guide to Long-Term Care Insurance*, publication no. 1262 (Washington, D.C.: Health Insurance Association of America, 1988), 2.

Chapter 2: Estate Planning

1. Lynne Ann DeSpelder and Albert Lee Strickland, *The Last Dance: Encountering Death and Dying* (Palo Alto, California: Mayfield Publishing Company, 1983), 300.
2. Alex J. Soled, *The Essential Guide to Wills, Estates, Trusts, and Death Taxes* (Glenview, Illinois: Scott, Foresman and Company; American Association of Retired Persons [AARP], 1984), 107.
3. Ibid., 144-5.

Chapter 3: Funeral Planning

1. *Why Pre-arrange (or Pre-fund) Funerals?* (Minneapolis, Minnesota: Minnesota Funeral Directors Association, 1984).
2. *Directory of Member Societies* (Washington, D.C.: The Continental Association of Funeral and Memorial Societies, 1988).
3. Merrill F. Unger, *Unger's Bible Dictionary* (Chicago, Illinois: Moody Press, 1957), 158-9.
4. Federal Trade Commission, *Facts for Consumers: Consumer Guide to the FTC Funeral Rule*, (Washington, D.C.: U.S. Government Printing Office, April 1984).
5. *What Do You Really Know About Funeral Costs?* (Milwaukee, Wisconsin: National Funeral Director's Association, 1974).
6. DeSpelder, *Last Dance*, 176-180.

Chapter 4: Coping With Death

1. Soled, *Guide to Wills*, 41.
2. Suzanne I. R. Hanson and Jude M. Eversley, *The Death of a Taxpayer* (Canada: CCH Canadian Limited, 1987), 7.
3. Ibid., 1.
4. Ibid., 4.
5. Ibid.
6. Ibid., 12.
7. Soled, *Guide to Wills*, 41.

8. Ruth Jean Loewinsohn, *Survival Handbook for Widows (and for relatives and friends who want to understand)*,(Glenview: Illinois: Scott, Foresman and Company, AARP, 1984) 57-8.

Chapter 5: Survivors' Benefits

1. Social Security Administration (SSA Publication No. 05-10084), *Survivors* (Washington, D.C.: U.S. Government Printing Office, Jan. 1989), 3-4.
2. Ibid., 9.
3. Ibid.
4. Veterans Administration, *Federal Benefits for Veterans and Dependents* (Washington, D.C.: U.S. Government Printing Office, IS-1 Fact Sheet, Jan. 1989), 37.
5. Ibid., 40.
6. Ibid.
7. Ibid., 42.
8. Ibid., 52.
9. Ibid., 62.
10. Ibid., 21.
11. Ibid., 28-33.
12. Ibid., 33-37.

Chapter 6: Housing Options

1. Oakley Hunter, *Forum III: Housing for the Retired* (Washington, D.C.: Federal National Mortgage Association, January, 1979), 11.
2. Michael Sumichrast, Ronald G. Shafer, and Marika Sumichrast, *Planning Your Retirement Housing* (Glenview, Illinois: Scott, Foresman and Company, AARP, 1984), 36-42.
3. Ibid., 95.
4. U.S. Department of Health and Human Services, *Where to Turn for Help for Older Persons* (Washington, D.C.: U.S. Government Printing Office, 1987) 8.
5. National Association of State Units on Aging, *What Is a State Unit On Aging?* (Washington, D.C.: U.S. Government Printing Office), 1-2.
6. Sumichrast, *Planning*, 95-6.
7. Ibid., 55.
8. Ibid., 56.
9. Ibid., 98.

10. *How to Plan Your Successful Retirement* (Glenview, Illinois: Scott, Foresman and Company; AARP, 1988), 79.
11. Sumichrast, *Planning*, 110.
12. Ibid., 104-6.
13. Ibid., 106-8.
14. *How to Buy a Manufactured Home* (Arlington, Virginia: Manufactured Housing Institute), 3.
15. Sumichrast, *Planning*, 114-7.
16. AARP, *Successful Retirement*, 81.
17. *Thinking About a Nursing Home?* (Washington, D.C.: American Health Care Association, 1988), 2-3.
18. U.S. Department of Health, *Where to Turn*, 12.
19. American Health Care Association, *Thinking About a Nursing Home?* 4.
20. Ibid., 5.
21. U.S. Department of Health, *Where to Turn*, 13-6.

Chapter 7: Grieving

1. DeSpelder, *Last Dance*, 193.
2. Miriam Baker Nye, *But I Never Thought He'd Die* (Philadelphia, Pennsylvania: The Westminster Press, 1978), 31-6.
3. Richard P. Walters, *Anger: Yours and Mine and What to Do About It* (Grand Rapids, Michigan: Zondervan Publishing Co., 1981), 23.

Glossary of Legal Terminology*

AdjustedGross Estate - The gross estate minus deductible funeral and administration expenses, claims against the estate, mortgages or indebtedness on property and losses not compensated for by insurance.

Administration Expenses - Those costs incurred in the administration of an estate.

Administration - The management of a decedent's estate by an executor, an administrator, a trustee, or a guardian.

Administrator - An individual or institution appointed by the court to administer and settle the estate of a person who dies without a will.

Administratrix - A female administrator.

Asset - All money, property, and money-related rights that someone owns.

Beneficiary - One who is designated to receive a benefit. A person who inherits under the terms of a will, or an individual or organization for whose benefit a trust is established.

Codicil - An amendment to a will executed with the same formalities as a will.

Contest - A challenge as to the validity of a will.

Decedent - A deceased person who is referred to as having died testate or intestate.

Estate - All of the property, both real and personal, owned by a person.

Estate Taxes - A tax imposed by the federal and the state government on the transfer of an individual's property (not the property itself) at his death and on certain other transfers deemed to be the equivalent of transfers at death.

Executor - An individual or organization (usually nominated by a testator) appointed by a court to carry out the terms of a will.

Exemption - An amount exempt from tax.

Gift Annuity - A transfer of property to a charitable organization, part of which is payment for an annuity and the balance of which is a charitable gift.

Gift Tax (Federal) - A tax imposed on the transfers of money or other property by gift during the calendar year or during a person's lifetime.

Gross Estate - Everything in which the decedent owned an interest at his death which is included in his estate for estate tax purposes. Items which may be included: life insurance, jointly owned property, transfers made in contemplation of death or intended to take effect after death, and the value of property in which the power to change the enjoyment of the property has been retained.

Heirs and Next-of-Kin - Individuals entitled to inherit the estate of a person who has died without a will under the laws of descent and distribution.

Holographic Will - A will written entirely in the maker's own handwriting.

Inheritance - An estate of a decedent which, in its restricted sense, is obtained by an individual through the laws of descent and distribution from an intestate, but, in its popular use, includes property obtained by devise or descent.

Inheritance Tax - A tax levied by some states on the transfer of property from a decedent at death. It is not a tax on the property itself but on the right to acquire it by descent or testamentary gift.

Instrument - A written document, a formal or legal document such as a contract or a will.

Intestacy - The state or condition of dying without having made a valid will or without having disposed by will of a part of the estate.

Intestate - Having died without a valid will or dying and leaving some property that is not covered by a will.

Jurisdiction - The authority by which a particular court (or other governmental unit) is empowered by statute to decide a certain kind of case and to have its decision enforced.

Legacy - A gift of money or personal property (anything but real estate which is a device) through a will.

Letters of Administration - The formal document evidencing the authority given to an administrator by a proper court to carry out the administration of an estate as prescribed by law (in the case of intestacy).

Letters Testamentary - The formal document evidencing the authority given to an executor by a proper court to carry out the administration of an estate as prescribed by law (in the case of a will).

Marital Deduction - The amount of money (currently unlimited) allowed for gifts of property given to a spouse during lifetime or passing to a surviving spouse upon death without paying estate or gift taxes).

Medicaid** - The joint state and federal program that states have adopted to provide payment for health care services to those with lower incomes or with very high medical bills. It does provide benefits for custodial and home health care once income and assets have been "spent down" to eligibility levels.

Medicare** - The federal program that is designed to provide those over age sixty-five, some disabled persons, and those with end-stage renal diseases with help in paying for hospital and medical expenses. It does not provide benefits for long-term care.

Medicaid Supplement Insurance (Medigap)** - Medigap is private insurance that supplements or fills in many of the gaps in Medicare coverage. It does not provide benefits for long-term care.

Order - A written command or direction given by a judge.

Personal Representative - A term used in some states to designate an executor or an administrator.

Power of Attorney - A document authorizing an individual to act on behalf of another individual.

Probate - The legal procedure by which a state court decrees that a will is genuine and executed in accordance with the formalities required by law. The term also refers to the process of administering a deceased person's estate.

Probate Estate - The assets held in a person's name at the time of his death which are subject to probate administration (as distinguished from assets in joint tenancy and life insurance).

Renunciation - The act by which a person abandons a right acquired without transferring it to another as, for example, the refusal of one who is named as an executor in a will to accept the appointment.

Revocable Trust - A trust agreement whereby the grantor retains the power to amend or terminate the trust.

Survivorship - The living of one of two or more persons after the death of the other or others.

Taxable Estate - The adjusted gross estate, minus any charitable and marital deductions available to the estate, upon which estate taxes are to be levied.

Taxable Income - The amount of income on which tax is computed — the result of subtracting from gross income all allowable deductions and exemptions.

Testamentary - Pertaining to a last will and testament or the administration of an estate (i.e., letters testamentary).

Testate - Having died with a valid will.

Testator or Testatrix - A person who makes a will. Testator refers to a man, and testatrix refers to a woman.

Totten Trust - A trust in the form of a bank account that passes to the named beneficiary upon the death of the grantor.

Trust - An arrangement whereby one person (the trustee) holds property for the benefit of another (the beneficiary). A trust provides specific instructions about the management and distribution of the property.

Trustee - The individual or institution that holds and manages the property of others according to the instructions given in a trust.

Trustor - The person who establishes a trust.

Unitrust - A charitable trust that provides for annual or more frequent payments to a person (or persons) measured by a fixed percentage (at least five percent) of the trust assets ultimately passing to a qualified charitable organization upon the death of the beneficiary (or benficiaries) or upon the expiration of a specified period of time.

Will - A legal instrument which is an expression or declaration of an individual's wishes concerning the disposition of his property after his death.

*Oran, Daniel, J.D., *Law Dictionary for Nonlawyers*, 2d ed. (St. Paul, Minnesota: West Publishing Company, 1985). All definitions are from this source unless otherwise stated.
** *The Consumer's Guide to Long-Term Care Insurance* (Washington, D.C.: Health Insurance Association of America), 10.

Bibliography

AARP Editors. *How to Plan Your Successful Retirement*. Glenview, Ill.: AARP Books; Scott, Foresman and Company; American Association of Retired Persons [AARP], 1988.

DeSpelder, Lynne Anne and Albert Lee Strickland. *The Last Dance: Encountering Death and Dying*. Mountain View, Calif.: Mayfield Publishing Company, 1983.

Graham, Billy. *Facing Death and the Life After*. Waco, Tex.: Word Books, 1987.

Grollman, Earl A. *Living When a Loved One Has Died*. Boston, Mass.: Beacon Press, 1977.

Hanson, Suzanne I. R. and Jude M. Eversley. *The Death of a Taxpayer*. Canada: CCH Canadian Limited, 1987.

Heavilin, Marilyn Willett. *Roses in December: Finding Strength Within Grief*. San Bernardino, Calif.: Here's Life Publishers, 1986.

Isle, Sherokee. *Empty Arms: Coping After Miscarriage, Stillbirth and Infant Deathcarriage, Stillbirth or Neonatal Death*: Long Lake, Minn.: Wintergreen Press, 1982.

Kubler-Ross, Elisabeth. *Death: The Final Stage of Growth*. New York: Touchstone Books, Simon & Schuster, 1986.

_____ . *On Death and Dying*. New York: Macmillan Publishing, 1970.

_____ . *Questions and Answers on Death and Dying*. New York: Macmillan Publishing, 1974.

Loewinsohn, Ruth Jean. *Survival Handbook for Widows (And for Relatives and Friends Who Want to Understand)*. Glenview, Ill.: Scott, Foresman and Company; [AARP], 1984.

Nelson, Thomas C. *It's Your Choice: The Practical Guide to Planning a Funeral.* Glenview, Ill.: Scott, Foresman and Company; [AARP], 1983.

Nye, Miriam Baker. *But I Never Thought He'd Die: Practical Help for Widows.* Louisville, Ky.. Westminster/John Knox Press, 1978.

Price, Eugenia. *Getting Through the Night: Finding Your Way After the Loss of a Loved One.* New York: Doubleday and Company, 1982.

Rank, Maureen. *Free to Grieve: Coping with the Trauma of Miscarriage.* Minneapolis: Bethany House Publishers, 1985.

Soled, Alex J. *Essential Guide to Wills, Estates, Trusts, and Death Taxes.* Glenview, Ill.: Scott, Foresman and Company; [AARP], 1984.

Sumichrast, Michael, Ronald G. Shafer, and Marika Sumichrast. *Planning Your Retirement Housing.* Glenview, Ill.: Scott, Foresman and Company; [AARP], 1984.

Veterans Administration. *Federal Benefits for Veterans and Dependents,* IS-1 Fact Sheet. Washington, D.C.: U.S. Government Printing Office, January 1989.

Walters, Richard P. *Anger: Yours and Mine and What to Do About It.* Grand Rapids, Mich.: Zondervan Publishing Co., 1981.

Watts, John G. *Leave Your House in Order.* Wheaton, Ill.: Tyndale House Publishers, 1979.

Yancey, Philip. *Where Is God When It Hurts?* Grand Rapids, Mich.: Zondervan, 1977.

If you would like additional information or would like to meet with one of our area representatives who would be happy to be of assistance at no obligation to you, please write to our office at the address below. We are here to serve you.

Development Ministries
Billy Graham Evangelistic Association
1300 Harmon Place
Minneapolis, MN 55403
(612) 338-0500

In Canada, write or call:

Development Ministries
Billy Graham Evangelistic Association of Canada
Box 841
Winnipeg, MB R3C 2R3
(204) 943-0529

Steps to Peace with God

Step 1 God's Purpose: Peace and Life

God loves you and wants you to experience peace and life—abundant and eternal.

The Bible Says . . .

". . . we have peace with God through our Lord Jesus Christ." Romans 5:1

"For God so loved the world that He gave His only begotten Son, that whoever believes in Him should not perish but have everlasting life." John 3:16

". . . I have come that they may have life, and that they may have it more abundantly." John 10:10b

Since God planned for us to have peace and the abundant life right now, why are most people not having this experience?

Step 2 Our Problem: Separation

God created us in His own image to have an abundant life. He did not make us as robots to automatically love and obey Him, but gave us a will and a freedom of choice.

We chose to disobey God and go our own willful way. We still make this choice today. This results in separation from God.

Our choice results in separation from God.

The Bible Says . . .

"For all have sinned and fall short of the glory of God." Romans 3:23

"For the wages of sin is death, but the gift of God is eternal life in Christ Jesus our Lord." Romans 6:23

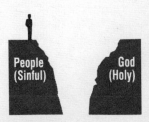

Our Attempts

Through the ages, individuals have tried in many ways to bridge this gap . . . without success . . .

The Bible Says . . .

"There is a way that seems right to man, but in the end it leads to death." Proverbs 14:12

"But your iniquities have separated you from God; and your sins have hidden His face from you, so that He will not hear." Isaiah 59:2

There is only one remedy for this problem of separation.

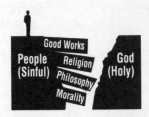

Step 3 God's Remedy: The Cross

Jesus Christ is the only answer to this problem. He died on the Cross and rose from the grave, paying the penalty for our sin and bridging the gap between God and people.

The Bible Says . . .

". . . God is on one side and all the people on the other side, and Christ Jesus, Himself man, is between them to bring them together . . ." 1 Timothy 2:5

"For Christ also has suffered once for sins, the just for the unjust, that He might bring us to God . . ." 1 Peter 3:18a

"But God demonstrates His own love for us in this: While we were still sinners, Christ died for us." Romans 5:8

God has provided the only way . . . we must make the choice . . .

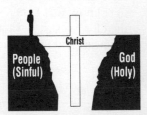

Step 4 | Our Response: Receive Christ

We must trust Jesus Christ and receive Him by personal invitation.

The Bible Says . . .

"**Behold, I stand at the door and knock. If anyone hears My voice and opens the door, I will come in to him and dine with him, and he with Me.**" **Revelation 3:20**

"**But as many as received Him, to them He gave the right to become children of God, even to those who believe in His name.**" **John 1:12**

"**. . . if you confess with your mouth the Lord Jesus and believe in your heart that God has raised Him from the dead, you will be saved.**" **Romans 10:9**

Are you here . . . or here?

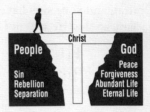

Is there any good reason why you cannot receive Jesus Christ right now?

How to receive Christ:

1. Admit your need (I am a sinner).
2. Be willing to turn from your sins (repent).
3. Believe that Jesus Christ died for you on the Cross and rose from the grave.
4. Through prayer, invite Jesus Christ to come in and control your life through the Holy Spirit. (Receive Him as Lord and Savior.)

What to Pray:

Dear Lord Jesus,

I know that I am a sinner and need Your forgiveness. I believe that You died for my sins. I want to turn from my sins. I now invite You to come into my heart and life. I want to trust and follow You as Lord and Savior.

In Jesus' name. Amen.

_____   _____
Date   Signature

God's Assurance:
His Word

If you prayed this prayer,
The Bible Says...

"For 'whoever calls upon the name of the Lord will be saved.'"
Romans 10:13

Did you sincerely ask Jesus Christ to come into your life? Where is He right now? What has He given you?

"For it is by grace you have been saved, through faith—and this is not from yourselves, it is the gift of God—not by works, so that no one can boast." Ephesians 2:8,9

The
Bible Says...

"He who has the Son has life; he who does not have the Son of God does not have life. These things I have written to you who believe in the name of the Son of God, that you may know that you have eternal life, and that you may continue to believe in the name of the Son of God."
1 John 5:12–13, NKJV

Receiving Christ, we are born into God's family through the supernatural work of the Holy Spirit who indwells every believer...this is called regeneration or the "new birth."

This is just the beginning of a wonderful new life in Christ. To deepen this relationship you should:

1. Read your Bible every day to know Christ better.
2. Talk to God in prayer every day.
3. Tell others about Christ.
4. Worship, fellowship, and serve with other Christians in a church where Christ is preached.
5. As Christ's representative in a needy world, demonstrate your new life by your love and concern for others.

God bless you as you do.

Billy Graham

If you want further help in the decision you have made, write to:
Billy Graham Evangelistic Association P.O. Box 779, Minneapolis, Minnesota 55440-0779